Collins

HISTORY

BOOK 2: 1750-1918

DERRICK MURPHY, MARK GOSLING, DAVE MARTIN

SERIES EDITOR: DERRICK MURPHY

Published by Collins Education
An imprint of HarperCollins Publishers
77–85 Fulham Palace Road
Hammersmith
London
W6 8JB

Browse the complete Collins catalogue at
www.collinseducation.com

HarperCollins Publishers Limited 2010
10 9 8 7 6 5 4 3 2 1

ISBN 978 0 00 7345755

British Library Cataloguing in Publication Data.
A Catalogue record for this publication is available from the British Library.

Commissioning Editors: Charlie Evans, Lucy McLoughlin
Project Editor: Tim Satterthwaite
Concept Design: EMC Design
Page Design: Ken Vail Graphic Design
Illustrations by Ken Vail Graphic Design
Cover Design by Joerg Hartmannsgruber, White-Card
Production: Simon Moore
Printed and bound by L.E.G.O. S.p.A., Italy

With particular thanks to Natalie Andrews.

Contents

The industrial age
Part 1: Britain 1750–1945

Objectives

By the end of this lesson you will be able to:

- describe some of the events and changes in the period 1750–1945
- explain some of the themes that run through these events

These three timelines show the events that took place between 1750 and 1945. The top bar shows how the government responded to the effects of industrialisation. The middle bar displays the political events that took place and the bottom bar shows the wars that occurred during this period.

1750	1760	1770	1780	1790	1800	1810	1820	1830

Industrialisation and Social reform

1830 Liverpool and Manchester Railway opened

1831 First cholera epidemic

1833 First of the Factory Acts

1834 Poor Law Act

1842 Mines Act

Political events

1819 Peterloo Massacre

1832 Reform Act. Allowed more people to vote

1839 Newport Rising

Wars

1756–63 Seven Years War

1775–82 American Revolutionary War

1789 French Revolution begins

1815 Battle of Waterloo

Century: one hundred years
Decade: ten years

Now it's your turn **APP**

At first glance, these timelines appear to be just lists of dates of events, but these can be sorted in a variety of ways.

1 Find all the dates connected with:
- the right of people to vote
- the development of the United Kingdom
- conflicts
- social reforms and the improvement of the lives of ordinary people
- the growth and the decline of the British Empire
- any other theme you can pick out
2 Can you think of any significant individuals associated with these events?
3 What other events do you think might also be included?

Check your progress

☆ I can describe some events.

☆☆ I can describe some of the events and why they happened.

☆☆☆ I can notice patterns between the different events.

0 | 1860 | 1870 | 1880 | 1890 | **1900** | 1910 | 1920 | 1930 | 1940 | **1950**

1870 Education Act. Councils had to build schools for all

1848 Second cholera epidemic

1848 Public Health Act

1867 Reform Act. Working class men gained the vote

1903 Suffragettes began campaigning

1918 Women over the age of 30 gained the vote

1947 Indian Independence and Partition

1872 Secret Ballot Act. Voting in secret put an end to bribery

1899–1902 South African War

1857 Indian Rebellion (also known as the Indian Mutiny)

1914–1918 World War One

1919–21 Irish War of Independence

1939–45 World War Two

Period: *a defined length of time, such as the Tudor period*

The industrial age
Part 2: How did life change in Britain from 1805 to 1925?

Objectives

By the end of this lesson you will be able to:

- describe what working people's homes were like at given points in time
- describe what changed and what stayed the same
- explain how people's lives changed over this period

Getting you thinking

Each of the four photographs A, B, C and D shows the interior of a terrace house. The terrace of cottages originally stood in Merthyr Tydfil in Wales. It was demolished, moved and rebuilt at the Welsh Folk Museum at St Fagan's. The interiors were then reconstructed by the *curators* to show life at a particular point in time. Each of the four labels 1805, 1855, 1895 and 1925 gives a little information about the family who actually lived in the houses at one point in time.

1805

The cottage is decorated as the home of a young family from west Wales working in the iron ore mine. As iron mine workers, they were quite well paid for the time. They were given their crude oak furniture as wedding presents. At this time people would have eaten from wooden bowls and cooked over the open fire.

1855

This is the home of Margaret Rosser, a 48 year-old widow. She was originally from Carmarthenshire. She made her living selling milk around the area. She had a 14 year-old daughter and sons aged 19 and 12, who both worked underground. This family ate from dishes and they had a clockwork spit for cooking.

1895

This is the home of William Richards, originally from Pembrokeshire, his wife, who was born in Merthyr, and their daughter. He was a railway signalman. Some of their furniture was mass-produced and had a smoother finish. Textiles make their house look cosier. They had a small oven.

1925

This is the home of a representative family and not a named one. This is because the museum staff believe that there is a moral issue involved. They do not think it is appropriate to reconstruct the homes of living people or people within living memory. Here the floor is covered with *linoleum* and the house now has running water.

Curator: a person who organises the displays in a museum

A

B

C

D

Now it's your turn APP

1 Your first task is to decide which label belongs to which of the four photographs A, B, C and D. You should find plenty of clues in the photographs to help you decide upon the chronological order.

2 Your second task is to compare each home with the one preceding it and to note down what has changed and what has stayed the same.

3 What can you learn from the photographs about how life changed in the period 1805 to 1925? Has life become more comfortable for working people? Has life become 'better'?

4 Do you agree with the museum staff's decision not to reconstruct the homes of living people or people within living memory?

Extension work

Compare the room in 1925 to your own living room at home. What are the differences? What is still the same?

Check your progress

I can describe what homes were like at different points in time.
I can describe how homes changed.
I can explain how life changed.

Linoleum: (lino), a floor covering made from linseed oil and resin, that was widely used after 1860

The industrial age
Part 3: People who made history – a case study

Many individuals have shaped historical events. These men and women have influenced modern British society. We are going to explore the impact of two people, Mary Seacole and David Lloyd George, on the development of Britain.

David Lloyd George

Mary Seacole

Getting you thinking

- In what ways do you think individuals can shape historical events?

In 1854 Britain went to war with Russia. The British feared the expansion of the Russian Empire into Eastern Europe. Fierce fighting took place in the Crimea in southern Russia. Thousands of British soldiers were killed and wounded. The hospitals and medical conditions provided for the soldiers were appalling. Mary Seacole, a West Indian nurse from Jamaica, travelled to London to offer her nursing skills. However, British authorities rejected her offer. Mary Seacole believed this was due to her skin colour.

Parliament: The British parliament is where laws are passed
House of Lords: one of the Houses of Parliament

Mary made her own way to the Crimea. She volunteered to work with Florence Nightingale but was rejected. She set up a company called Seacole and Day and established the 'British Hotel' close to the fighting in Balaclava. She provided British troops with food and medical supplies, and nursed wounded soldiers. After the war she returned to England *bankrupt*. However, soldiers raised funds to help her survive. She wrote a popular book about her experiences. This book made people more aware of the need to improve the treatment of injured soldiers.

David Lloyd George was a Liberal Party politician. His actions had a lasting impact on Britain. He supported a health insurance scheme in 1911. The scheme helped a worker's family if the worker became ill. In 1911 Lloyd George supported the passing of the *Parliament* Act. The *House of Lords* lost the power to stop '*money bills*'. Lloyd George wanted to raise taxes to help poor people improve their lives. Many wealthy men in the House of Lords opposed this idea.

Lloyd George's political influence increased during World War One. In December 1916, Herbert Asquith, the prime minister, resigned over criticisms of his leadership. In 1915, there had been ammunition shortages, which Lloyd George helped solve. In December 1916, public support for Lloyd George increased and he became prime minister. The war ended in 1918 with victory for Britain.

After the war, Lloyd George became involved in negotiations over the future of Ireland. In 1921, Lloyd George agreed to the establishment of the Irish Free State and Northern Ireland.

Now it's your turn

In what ways did Mary Seacole and David Lloyd George have an impact on the development of Britain?

Check your progress

I can place the lives of Mary Seacole and David Lloyd George in chronological order.
I can describe some of their actions.
I can explain why the actions of Mary Seacole and David Lloyd George were important.

Money bill: A law which involves spending money for the country
Bankrupt: no longer having money to pay debts

How did the Industrial Revolution change the lives of ordinary people?

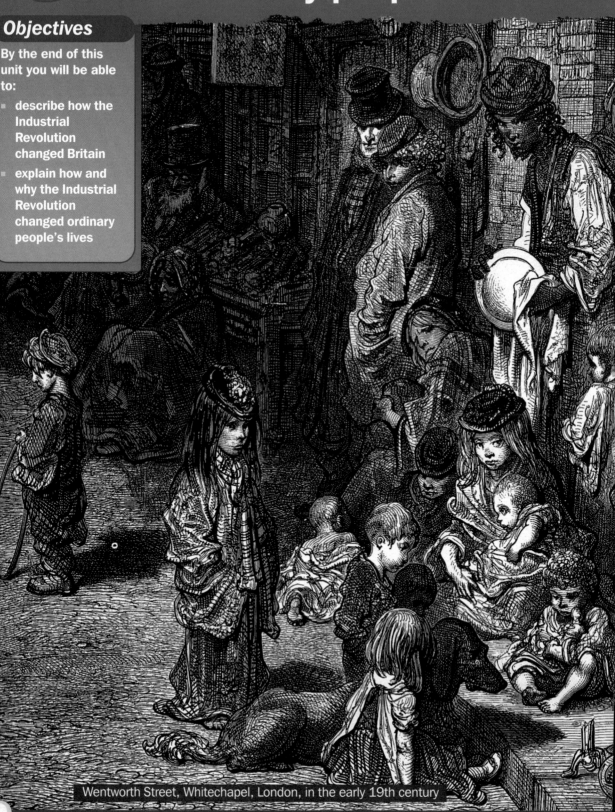

Wentworth Street, Whitechapel, London, in the early 19th century

The Industrial Revolution was one of the most important periods of British industry. Britain changed from a country where most people worked in agriculture to a country where most people worked in industry. This change also involved a major movement in population from the countryside to towns.

Look at the image. It shows a street in an industrial town in nineteenth-century Britain. The houses are close together. The street is crowded with people. Look at how the people are dressed. The street has been shaped by the changes brought about by the Industrial Revolution.

People moved to towns in order to work in factories. These factories produced manufactured goods such as cloth and machinery. The working and living conditions in many industrial towns were poor. People worked long hours for low pay. Even children worked in factories and many did not attend school. Towns lacked ways of getting rid of rubbish. They also lacked a clean water supply. The crowded living conditions in towns led to the growth of disease. This led to a high level of illness, with many children dying from disease when they were very young.

Questions

1 Describe what you can see in the picture.
2 What message do you think the image gives about life in an industrial town in the nineteenth century?
3 Can you explain how the Industrial Revolution affected living conditions for many ordinary people?

Who had the greatest impact – Abraham Darby or Richard Arkwright?

Objectives

By the end of this unit you will be able to:

- describe the work of Richard Arkwright and Abraham Darby
- decide who had the greatest impact

The Industrial Revolution was a period of rapid changes in industry. You are going to meet two of the men who made it happen.

Getting you thinking

The Industrial Revolution was possible because of the money from farming improvements. There were many changes, but perhaps the biggest was the development of factories and iron works. These employed many workers together in one place, instead of in their own homes as had happened before.

Richard Arkwright (1732–1792)

Richard Arkwright

Arkwright was a businessman who saw an opportunity to make money in the *textile industry*. He provided money for an inventor who developed a machine for spinning cotton. The machine produced a better thread than existing machines. As it was so big, it required power to drive it and a large space to put it in: a factory. Arkwright decided to use water power, and the machine became known as the 'water frame'.

In 1771 Arkwright borrowed enough money to open the first cotton factory at Cromford, by the river Derwent. To attract workers, Arkwright built cottages close to the factory, and people came from around Derbyshire. He preferred weavers with large families. The women and children (from age six) worked in his spinning factory. The men worked at home weaving the thread into cloth.

The mill was successful and Arkwright built more in Lancashire, Staffordshire and Scotland. From these mills and the *patents* he took out, he made a fortune. He is sometimes called the 'father of the factory system'.

Textile industry: the making of woollen or cotton cloth on a large scale
Patent: a legal document that stops anyone else copying your ideas

Abraham Darby I
(1678–1717)

Darby was a *Quaker* businessman who saw an opportunity in the iron-making industry. He was making brass pots in Bristol but as these were too expensive, he changed to iron pots instead. One of his workers solved the technical problems of casting iron by using dry sand for the mould. Darby took out a patent on this.

Darby moved his business and his workers to Coalbrookdale in Shropshire. This was close to the coalfields and there was already a blast furnace that he could lease and adapt. Here he developed a method of producing high quality iron in a blast furnace. He used coke made from the local coal rather than charcoal as fuel. This was a major advance. It allowed large quantities of iron to be produced. This iron was the material that the Industrial Revolution would need most. Darby's iron went into steam engines, bridges and machines: the inventions that made Britain so successful in the nineteenth century.

The first iron bridge at Coalbrookdale, built with Darby iron. There are no portraits of Abraham Darby I, as the Quaker religion discourages images of people

Now it's your turn

1 Which of these two men had the greatest impact on the Industrial Revolution?
2 If you were going to 'tweet' a friend summing up their contribution, what would it say?

Check your progress

I can describe who Darby and Arkwright were.
I can summarise their achievements.
I can explain who had the greatest impact, and give reasons.

Tweet: a Twitter message of just 140 characters, including spaces and punctuation!
Quaker: A religious group which opposed violence

Rural life on the eve of industrial change

Objectives

By the end of this lesson you will be able to:

- describe what Britain was like on the eve of the Industrial Revolution
- use travellers' accounts to find out about Aylesford in Kent

Today most of us live in towns and cities, but this was not always the case.

The picture below is a view of Aylesford, near Maidstone in Kent, in the early nineteenth century. What words or phrases would you use to describe the scene?

Getting you thinking

In 1750 the population of Britain was about 11 million. About 80 per cent – that is eight out of every ten people – lived in the countryside, in small places like Aylesford. The most important work was farming, but was there any other economic activity?

Fortunately, the accounts of two visitors to the area survive.

Aylesford, Kent, in the early nineteenth century

'From Kent, and particularly from that part which lies this way; they bring the large Kentish bullocks, famed for being generally all red, and with their horns crooked inward, the two points standing one directly against the other, they are counted the largest breed in England.

From the same country are brought great quantities of the largest timber for supply of the king's yards at Chatham, and often to London; most of which comes by land carriage to Maidstone.

From the country adjoining to Maidstone also, is a very great quantity of corn brought up to London, besides hops and cherries.

Also a kind of paving stone, about eight to ten inches square, so durable that it scarce ever wears out; 'tis used to pave courtyards, and passages to gentlemen's houses.

Also fine white sand for the glass-houses, thought the best in England for melting into flint-glass, and looking glass-plates; and for the stationer's use also, vulgarly called writing-sand.'

Also very great quantities of fruit, such as Kentish pippins and runetts which come up as the cherries do, whole hoy-loads at a time to the wharf, called the Three Cranes, in London; which is the greatest pippin market perhaps in the world.'

Source 1 *A tour thro' the whole island of Great Britain,* Daniel Defoe, 1724–7

We entered Aylesford by a steep old Stone Bridge; and so to The Anchor Ale House, as bad a stop as could be, with most miserable stabling. The Day was so gay that any misery was to be Endured—so we attempted to be happy over our bad mutton chops and a Pudding with Brandy and Water. We saw, whilst at Dinner, a Gang of well-mounted smugglers pass by: How often have I wished to be able to purchase a Horse from their excellent Stables.—No Dinner could be worse than ours; nor could a stupider Inn Keeper be found!

Source 2 *A Tour of Kent,* John Byng, 1790

Now it's your turn

From information provided in the sources, answer the following questions.

1 What food items were produced in Kent? Where were they sold?
2 What industries were supplied from Kent?
3 What illegal trade went on?
4 How were people and goods transported?

Check your progress

I can use travellers' tales as evidence of nineteenth century life.
I can describe aspects of *rural* life in Kent.
I can talk about what Britain was like before the Industrial Revolution.

Rural: to do with the countryside

Why was the farmland enclosed?

Objectives

By the end of this lesson you will be able to:

- explain why land was enclosed
- describe what effect the changes had on villages
- understand what the effects of enclosure were

When we are out in the countryside, we expect to see the land divided into fields by hedges and fences – but it was not always like this.

An aerial photograph of fields in Scotland, showing the traces of older kinds of farming

Enclosure: the fencing in of land for arable farming (growing crops) or for animal breeding

Getting you thinking

- Are there more people living in Britain now than in the past? When and why do you think Britain's population started to increase?

Between 1750 and 1825, the population of Britain almost doubled. At the same time more and more people were living in towns. This created a demand for more food, and landowners saw an opportunity to make money. But first they needed to reorganise the way land was used. To do this they asked parliament for an *Enclosure* Act, and as the members of parliament were also from the landowning class, these acts were passed. Between 1750 and 1860, approximately 5,000 individual acts were passed, and over seven million acres of land were enclosed. That was roughly 21 per cent of England, so it was a significant process, but it is important to remember that not everywhere was affected. In some places enclosure had already happened in Tudor times.

Now it's your turn

1 Look closely at the photograph. What can you see? Can you see evidence of older shapes that have now almost disappeared? What do you think these shapes might be?
2 Can you find a field with a series of faint lines running across it? What do you think these lines might be?
3 What do you think might have caused these things to change?

Village life before enclosure

Before enclosure, most people in a typical English village were labourers who worked for the local landowner. Even those who did not own any land had the right to graze their cattle, sheep and geese on the common and to collect firewood. In their cottage gardens they would grow vegetables, and might keep pigs and chickens.

In the open fields the same crops were grown as had been grown in medieval times. In many villages, one third of the land was left fallow to recover its goodness each year. On the common land, people's animals were mixed together.

Village life after enclosure

After enclosure, all the land of the village – including the common – was divided up amongst all those who owned land. Those who owned no land lost their right to use the common. In the enclosed fields, a farmer could grow whatever crop he wished, without needing the agreement of his neighbours. And he could graze just his own animals, so that he could control their breeding.

Check your progress

★ I can explain what enclosure was.
★★ I can describe some of the effects of enclosure.
★★★ I can explain how enclosure affected people in different ways.

Local history

Was farmland in your local area enclosed? One clue to look out for is fields with straight boundaries (hedges or fences) and straight roads and farm tracks.

Which of the changes in agriculture were more important?

Objectives

By the end of this unit you will be able to:

- describe the changes in agriculture
- explain which changes were more important

Fencing in the land led to changes in farming, but as you will see, that was not all that was affected.

Getting you thinking

Enclosure allowed those who wanted to make improvements to do so. These fall into two main areas, arable farming – growing crops, and pastoral farming – rearing animals.

- Can you name some of the crops that are grown today by Britain's farmers, and some of the animals that are reared?

Arable farming

New crops and rotations

In the old three-field system, wheat and barley were grown in two of the fields; the third was left fallow or planted with *legumes*. Every year, each crop moved on one field. In 1730, Charles Townshend introduced a new four-field *crop rotation* that he had seen used in Flanders (present-day Belgium), which allowed all the land to be used each year. This included the growing of turnips and clover. The advantage was that the turnips provided food for animals, and the animals' dung could be used as fertilizer for the soil. This meant more animals could be bred and the grain yields were higher. Townshend's pioneering work was copied by others. So the farmers made bigger profits.

A Shorthorn cow, one of the new breeds developed in the eighteenth century

Legumes: any plant of the pea family, used to improve the soil

Improved drainage

Another improvement came from Flanders. Flemish engineers with experience of improving field drainage were employed by English farmers to make their land more productive. This land could then either be farmed more profitably or rented out for higher rents. Either way landowners made more money and more food was grown.

Mechanisation

A number of technological innovations were introduced. Jethro Tull's seed drill planted seeds more efficiently. John Small's improved iron plough turned the soil more effectively. The effect of these inventions was to improve crop yields and therefore increase profits. Andrew Meikle's threshing machine was more controversial. This cut the number of farm labourers needed for threshing. This led to the Swing Riots in the 1830s, where farm labourers smashed machines.

Pastoral farming

Selective stock breeding

The most famous pioneer of this was Robert Bakewell. He crossed Longhorn with Lincoln sheep to produce a new breed, New Leicester sheep. These put on weight quickly and so farmers made more money from rearing them. Other breeders produced improved varieties of pigs and cattle.

Charles Darwin, writing in the middle of the nineteenth century, was influenced by selective breeding. The first chapter of his famous book, *On the Origin of Species,* was about the selective breeding of cattle and other animals.

Agricultural improvements led to higher rents and profits. Some of these were invested in further improvements and in industry, thus making the Industrial Revolution possible. They also led to a decrease in demand for agricultural labour, particularly for women's work. People moved to the towns in search of work and found it in the new factories.

Now it's your turn

1 List the changes that affected
   • farming
   • people's lives
   • ideas
2 Which of the changes you have listed do you think were most important, and why?

Check your progress

I can describe some of the changes in agriculture.
I can describe some changes for life in the countryside.
I can explain which changes were most important, and give reasons.

What was it like to work in a cotton mill?

One key change of the Industrial Revolution was that people had to go to the factory to work instead of working at home.

Getting you thinking

The new textile factories and iron works needed all their workers to start and finish at the same time every day. This was a new experience for adults and children; beforehand no one had such strict control over the hours people worked. This meant workers lost the freedom to start and finish when they wished that they used to enjoy when they worked in their own homes. Whilst the working hours and conditions might have been no worse than they had been used to in their own homes, many workers missed this loss of freedom.

For the employers too, the factory system was new. They had invested large sums of money in the buildings and machines. So they believed they needed to keep their factory and machines running for as long as possible to ensure they made a profit. They also had to develop ways of managing all their workers, who were now concentrated in one place. Having factory rules was one way to do this. The rules they established can tell us a lot about what life was like in a cotton mill and what the mill owners were concerned about.

Now it's your turn

Study the list of rules on the right. Some were designed to make the mill run productively, some were about the quality of the cloth being produced (especially its cleanness), some were about careful use and maintenance of the machinery, and some were about the workers' behaviour. Can you decide which rules belong in which category?

Factory rules in a cotton mill owned by Whitakers and Sons, Yorkshire, 1851.

✴ Any person arriving late for work will be fined as follows:
  5 minutes' late: 2d
  10 minutes' late: 4d
  15 minutes' late: 6d

✴ Any person leaving waste on the floor fined 2d.

✴ Any use of bad language will be fined 3d for the first offence and for any other offence will be dismissed.

✴ All the machinery must be cleaned at every meal break.

✴ All persons in our employ shall serve Four Weeks' Notice before leaving their employ: but L. WHITAKERS & Sons, shall and will turn any person off without notice being given.

✴ Any person wilfully or negligently breaking the Machinery, they shall pay for the same to its full value.

✴ The Masters would recommend that all their workpeople Wash themselves every morning, but they shall Wash themselves at least twice every week, Monday Morning and Thursday morning; and any found not washed will be fined 3d for each offence.

Check your progress

★ I can use a source to describe working life in a cotton mill.
★★ I can explain what the rules reveal about the factory owners' concerns.
★★★ I can describe some differences between the factory system and the way people worked before the Industrial Revolution.

Children working in factories

Objectives

By the end of this unit you will be able to:

- explain how children were treated in cotton mills
- decide if you think *legislation* was necessary

Getting you thinking

Life in a factory in early nineteenth-century Britain was very harsh. People had to work very long hours for low wages. It was normal for people to work 10 to 12 hours six days a week. Usually factory workers got Sunday off to allow them to go to church!

Today all children are meant to go to school until they are 16 years of age. In the early nineteenth century many children went to work. Their parents needed this because it brought in extra money to the home.

Also, factory owners liked to employ children. They were paid less than adults and could be bullied into working hard. Children worked around machines that were highly dangerous, and were often injured. The sources on the right, which are from a parliamentary enquiry, reveal the hardship of children working in factories.

Clarence Mill, Bollington, built in the nineteenth century

Legislation: the passing of new laws by parliament

Eliza Marshall

Q What were your hours of work?

A When I first went to the mill, we worked from six in the morning till seven in the evening. After a time, we began at five in the morning, and worked till ten at night.

Q Were you very much fatigued by that length of labour?

A Yes.

Q Did they beat you?

A When I was younger they used to do it often.

Q Did the labour affect your limbs?

A Yes, when we worked over-hours I was worse by a great deal; I had stuff to rub my knees

Q Were you straight before that?

A Yes, I was; my master knows that well enough.

Q Are you crooked now?

A Yes, I have an iron on my leg; my knee is contracted.

Dr Samuel Smith

Q Is not the labour in mills and factories 'light and easy'?

A It is often described as such, but I do not agree at all with that definition. The exertion required from them is considerable, and, in all the instances with which I am acquainted, the whole of their labour is performed in a standing position.

Q What are the effects of this on the children?

A Up to twelve or thirteen years of age, the bones are so soft that they will bend in any direction. By long continued standing the knees become so weak that they turn inwards, producing that deformity which is called "knock-knees" and I have sometimes seen it so striking, that the individual has actually lost twelve inches of his height by it.

Q Are there many accidents in the factories and mills?

A I have frequently seen accidents of the most dreadful kind. I have seen cases in which the arm had been torn off near the shoulder joint; I have seen the upper extremity chopped into small fragments, from the tip of the finger to above the elbow.

Now it's your turn

Eliza was one witness questioned by Michael Sadler's House of Commons committee. It was set up in 1832 to investigate child labour. Does her evidence and that of the other witnesses convince you that laws were needed to regulate the employment of children? You might consider their age, hours and safety.

David Rowland

Q At what age did you commence working in a cotton mill?

A Just when I had turned six.

Q What employment had you in a mill in the first instance?

A That of a scavenger.

Q Will you explain the nature of the work that a scavenger has to do?

A The scavenger has to take the brush and sweep under the wheels. I frequently had to be under the wheels, and in consequence of the perpetual motion of the machinery, I was liable to accidents constantly. I was very frequently obliged to lie flat, to avoid being run over or caught.

Check your progress

I can use a source to describe the work of children in factories.

I can explain some of the dangers of working in factories.

I can explain why legislation was needed to protect children.

Working in the coal mines

Objectives

By the end of this unit you will be able to:

- describe what conditions were like in coal mines
- decide if you think legislation was necessary

It was not just cotton mills where working conditions were bad; coal mines were also very dangerous. People working in coal mines experienced dark, wet and cramped conditions. They also faced hazards such as explosions, suffocating gases and flooding.

Getting you thinking

The sources on the right are taken from another report, into conditions in coal mines. What was Sarah Goober, one of the people questioned, most bothered about?

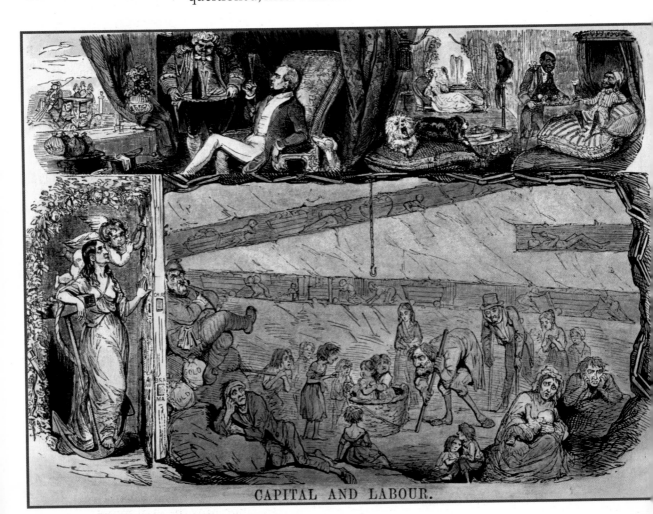

'Capital and Labour', cartoon, 1843

26

Now it's your turn

Increased demand for coal led to more and deeper mines. These attracted the attention of reformers. In 1842 Lord Shaftesbury led a royal commission to investigate the employment of women and children underground.

1 Sarah was one child who gave evidence. Read her account, and that of the other witnesses. What problems can you identify?

2 Does their evidence convince you that laws were needed to regulate the employment of women and children underground?

I'm a trapper in the Gawber pit. It does not tire me, but I have to trap without a light and I'm scared. I go at four and sometimes half past three in the morning, and come out at five and half past. I never go to sleep. Sometimes I sing when I've light, but not in the dark; I dare not sing then. I don't like being in the pit. I am very sleepy when I go sometimes in the morning. I go to Sunday-schools and read Reading made Easy.

Source 1 *Sarah Gooder, a mine worker*

I carry about one hundred weight and a quarter on my back; have to stoop much and creep through water, which is frequently up to the calves of my legs. When first down fell frequently asleep while waiting for coal from heat and fatigue.

I do not like the work, nor do the lassies, but they are made to like it. When the weather is warm there is difficulty in breathing, and frequently the lights go out.

Source 2 *Isabella Read*

I have worked down in pit five years; father is working in next pit; I have 12 brothers and sisters; I *hurry* for my brother John, and come down at seven o'clock about; I go up at six, sometimes seven; I do not like working in pit, but I am obliged to get a living; I work always without stockings, or shoes, or trousers; I wear nothing but my chemise; I have to go up to the headings with the men; they are all naked there; I am got well used to that, and don't care now much about it; I was afraid at first, and did not like it; they never behave rudely to me; I cannot read or write.

Source 3 *Mary Barrett*

The employment of females of any age in the mines is most objectionable, and I should rejoice to see it put an end to; but in the present feeling of the colliers, no individual would succeed in stopping it in a neighbourhood where it prevailed, because the men would immediately go to those pits where their daughters would be employed.

Source 4 *Thomas Wilson, mine owner*

Check your progress

★ I can describe the work of women and children in coal mines.

★★ I can describe some of the hazards coal miners faced.

★★★ I can suggest some of the reasons why it was difficult to change how the coal mines were run.

Hurry: to pull coal in a cart underground from coalface to the lift shaft

What was changed by the factory acts?

As a result of the work of reformers, parliament began to pass laws to deal with some of the problems that had been discovered.

Pictures of cotton mills, showing children working near and underneath machinery

Getting you thinking

Look at the illustrations. What hazards can you see for the factory workers?

Not everyone agreed with factory reform. Some owners resented the government telling them how to run their businesses. Many believed that the more hours their factory was running, the more profits they would make. When the hours of children were cut, they used the relay system. The men could work much longer hours so children worked in relays to keep the factories running.

Some workers resented losing their employment or the wages that their wives and children could earn. We should remember that before the factory system was developed men, women and children often worked very long hours in their own homes; and sometimes in very poor working conditions.

Now it's your turn

Look at the timeline, which lists most of the major acts that were passed by parliament, and some of the changes that were required by the acts.

1 How might factory owners or factory workers have evaded these requirements?
2 Why do you think the Civil Registration Act needed to be passed?
3 Study the timeline and identify changes in the following areas:
   • the age at which children could start working
   • the hours that children could work
   • the hours that women could work
   • efforts to enforce the acts

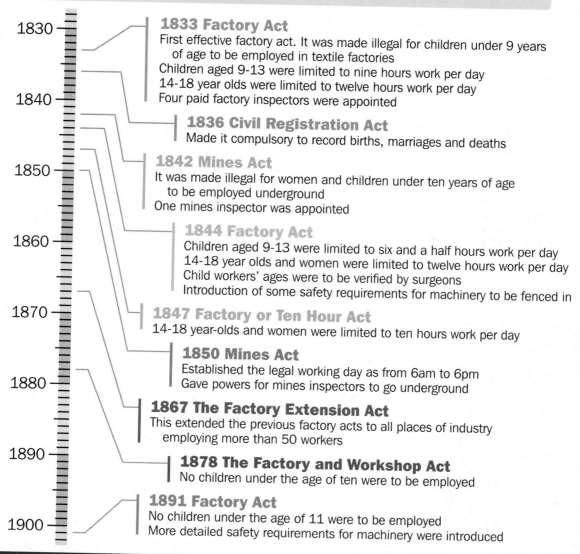

1833 Factory Act
First effective factory act. It was made illegal for children under 9 years of age to be employed in textile factories
Children aged 9-13 were limited to nine hours work per day
14-18 year olds were limited to twelve hours work per day
Four paid factory inspectors were appointed

1836 Civil Registration Act
Made it compulsory to record births, marriages and deaths

1842 Mines Act
It was made illegal for women and children under ten years of age to be employed underground
One mines inspector was appointed

1844 Factory Act
Children aged 9-13 were limited to six and a half hours work per day
14-18 year olds and women were limited to twelve hours work per day
Child workers' ages were to be verified by surgeons
Introduction of some safety requirements for machinery to be fenced in

1847 Factory or Ten Hour Act
14-18 year-olds and women were limited to ten hours work per day

1850 Mines Act
Established the legal working day as from 6am to 6pm
Gave powers for mines inspectors to go underground

1867 The Factory Extension Act
This extended the previous factory acts to all places of industry employing more than 50 workers

1878 The Factory and Workshop Act
No children under the age of ten were to be employed

1891 Factory Act
No children under the age of 11 were to be employed
More detailed safety requirements for machinery were introduced

Check your progress

★   I can describe some of the changes in the Factory Acts.
★★   I can explain why these changes were made.
★★★   I am able to find some patterns in the ways changes came about.

What was life like in the new industrial towns?

Objectives

By the end of this unit you will:

- know why people moved into towns
- be able to explain how quickly towns grew

One feature of the Industrial Revolution was the rapid growth of towns.

Getting you thinking

Study the woodcut, by an artist called Gustave Doré. What problems of living in a town can you see?

A London slum under a railway bridge, woodcut by Gustave Doré

People moved into towns for a number of reasons. There were jobs in the new factories and industries. There were jobs in the trades supporting the population in towns, such as building houses or supplying food. In the countryside there was poverty and unemployment, as new methods and machines meant that farming required fewer workers. Wages in farming were low. The town offered the promise of excitement and new opportunities. And the growth of the railways made movement quicker and easier.

As towns grew a number of problems developed. There was an increased demand for houses. This led to overcrowding in existing houses. It was also an opportunity for developers to build new housing for rent. These new houses were not always well planned or well built. As the towns grew larger, the existing systems for running them began to collapse. Rubbish might be uncollected or clean water not available. This affected the health of many people, and life expectancy was low.

Population figures (in thousands) for towns 1750–1851

	1750	1801	1851
Birmingham	24	71	233
Bradford	4	13	104
Bristol	22	61	137
Glasgow	32	77	357
Liverpool	22	82	376
Manchester	17	75	303

Note: figures for 1750 are estimates but all others are based upon the official *census* data.

In 1842 the government conducted an investigation into the living conditions of British people. They found that the average life expectancy of labourers in urban Liverpool was just 15 years old, whereas in rural Wiltshire it was 33. Similarly, wealthy professionals in rural Rutland could live, on average, to 52, while in Manchester the average life expectancy was 38.

Now it's your turn

1 Can you suggest any reasons why people felt they must move to towns?
2 After looking at the figures for population do you think towns underwent a rapid or steady growth?
3 During which 50-year period do you think the population growth was the fastest? Can you suggest why this was?
4 Can you see any patterns between where people lived, their occupations, and average life expectancy?
5 Now study the woodcut by Doré. Apart from overcrowding, what other problems do you think there might have been in the growing towns and cities?

Check your progress

★ I can use numerical data as evidence for population growth.
★★ I can explain the pattern between occupation and life expectancy.
★★★ I can explain why towns grew.

Census: a survey of the population of a country or place, carried out every ten years in the United Kingdom

Life in the slums

Objectives

By the end of this unit you will be able to:

- list some problems of the growing towns
- explain why they were unhealthy places

Now let's have a closer look at the health problems in the growing industrial towns.

Getting you thinking

Study the cartoon. What are the hazards of town life, according to the cartoonist?

You will have seen from the life expectancy discussion in the previous lesson that the poorer a person was, the more likely they were to die young. This is because the problems in the poorer parts of the growing industrial towns and cities were much more severe. And the local government system was unable to deal with them.

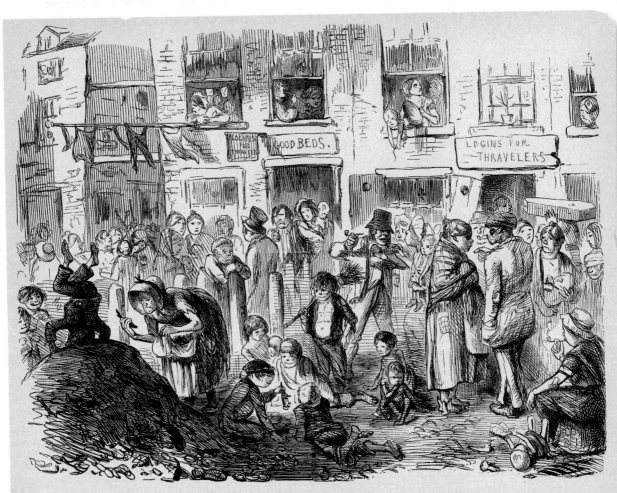

A COURT FOR KING CHOLERA.

'A *Court* for King Cholera', *Punch* magazine, 5 September 1852, showing life in a Victorian slum

Cholera: an often fatal disease spread by bacteria in contaminated water
Privy: toilet   *Court: an enclosed square surrounded by houses*

Overcrowding of houses and within houses

There was no town planning so new houses could be built with little thought for drainage, sewage, water supply or street paving. All of these had an impact on the health of those living in the houses.

Within the houses themselves there was overcrowding, as families shared and took in lodgers in order to afford the rent. This meant that any disease could spread quickly.

Poor quality housing

Builders were keen to make money from renting out property and so the new houses were often poorly built with earth floors, single brick walls and flimsy roofs. This meant they were often damp and this, added to the lack of ventilation, led to breathing-related diseases.

Drinking water

Most houses did not have piped water. Their water might be taken from public pumps and wells, or from streams and rivers. All of these might be polluted by the town's waste and so be a source of disease, especially *cholera*.

Rubbish

In many towns there was no system for collecting rubbish. Piles of rotting rubbish were a breeding ground for disease.

Sewage

Most houses were built without sewers or toilets. Houses usually shared a *privy* which might be built over a stream, but which was more likely to be over a *cesspit*. There were two problems with these. Often they were unlined so the sewage could seep into the water supply. Secondly, if they were not regularly emptied then there was a danger of them overflowing.

General cleanliness and hygiene

The lack of water meant that people found it difficult to keep themselves, their clothing and their homes clean. This created ideal conditions for diseases to spread.

Now it's your turn

Cartoons were important sources of information. They revealed much about the conditions of Britain's towns, and allowed the cartoonist to criticise through exaggeration.

1 John Leech drew 'A Court for King Cholera'; how far do you think he was exaggerating the conditions of the poor?
2 Which of the problems listed on this page has Leech included?
3 Which one is missing?

Check your progress

I can describe some of the problems of the growing industrial towns.
I can explain the link between these problems and people's health.
I can explain why cartoonists were important.

Cesspit: a deep pit used to dispose of sewage or rubbish

Killer in the water

Poor conditions in the growing towns allowed disease to spread, but the biggest killer was cholera.

Getting you thinking

Cholera arrived from Russia in 1831. The first victim died in Sunderland. By the end of 1832, over 32,000 people had died. The disease was particularly horrifying because it spread so quickly.

- Why do you think cholera spread so quickly?

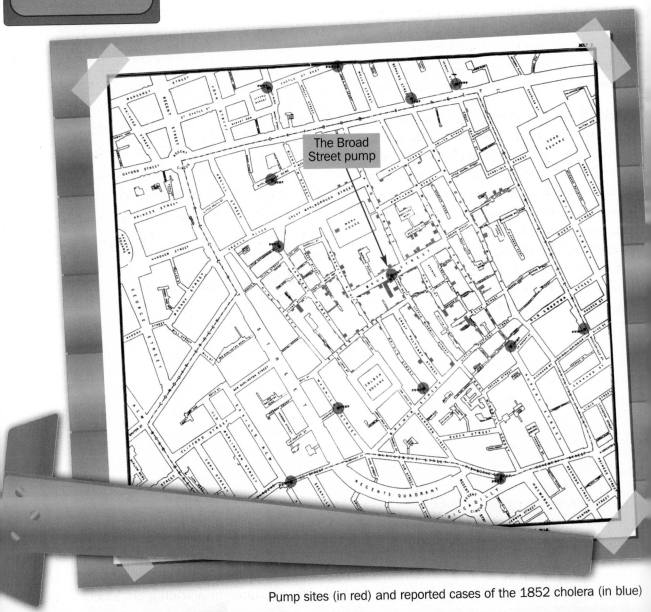

The Broad Street pump

Pump sites (in red) and reported cases of the 1852 cholera (in blue)

Cholera victims died quickly and with great suffering; and cholera killed both rich and poor. The government's response was to allow towns to set up Boards of Health. The belief was that cholera was caused by bad air, so these boards cleaned the streets and lime-washed houses. Some also improved sewage and water supply. However, as the disease did not reoccur, these boards were dissolved and people forgot. And many believed that government had no business interfering in people's lives or spending money on improvements.

One man, Edwin Chadwick, did not forget. In 1842 he produced a shocking report on conditions in towns. The government listened and agreed with his conclusions, but there were still many people opposed. It was difficult to order towns to make improvements. That all changed in 1848 when a second cholera epidemic killed over 50,000 people. The 1848 Public Health Act was passed, which made towns improve sewage systems. But one major problem remained: What caused cholera?

John Snow found the answer. In 1852–53 a third cholera epidemic killed over 10,000 people in London alone. But it was here that Snow was able to make the link between cholera and water supply, as Source 1 shows. Even then it took over 25 years before his findings were accepted. The Public Health Act, making it a requirement in law for local authorities to provide clean water, was not passed until 1875.

> I found that nearly all the deaths had taken place within a short distance of the [Broad Street] pump. There were only ten deaths in houses situated decidedly nearer to another street-pump. In five of these cases the families of the deceased persons informed me that they always sent to the pump in Broad Street, as they preferred the water to that of the pumps which were nearer. In three other cases, the deceased were children who went to school near the pump in Broad Street...
>
> With regard to the deaths occurring in the locality belonging to the pump, there were 61 instances in which I was informed that the deceased persons used to drink the pump water from Broad Street, either constantly or occasionally...

Source 1 Extract from Snow's letter to the Medical Times

Now it's your turn

1 Why was cholera so feared as a disease?
2 Why did it take so long for towns to provide clean water and sewage systems?
3 How did Chadwick and Snow help to produce this change?

Check your progress

☆ I can describe some of the public health changes.
☆☆ I can suggest why they took so long to happen.
☆☆☆ I can explain the importance of Chadwick and Snow in defeating cholera.

The age of the canal

Objectives

By the end of this lesson you will be able to:

- describe how canals helped Britain become a more wealthy country
- give reasons why canals were difficult to build

At the beginning of eighteenth century, the only way to transport goods and raw materials across Britain was by dirt road. These were badly maintained and became almost unusable in bad weather. Britain needed a way to transport bulky goods across the country at low cost. The development of man-made canals was the answer.

Getting you thinking

- Have you ever been on a canal? What do you think they were built for?

During the eighteenth century Britain began to develop industry. The textile machine-making industry of Birmingham and the pottery industry of Stoke needed a cheap and easy way to get raw materials. They also needed a way to transport their finished goods for sale.

Drawn by Thos. H. Shepherd.   Engraved by F. J. Havell.

THE DOUBLE LOCK, & EAST ENTRANCE
TO THE ISLINGTON TUNNEL, REGENT'S CANAL.
TO COLONEL DRINKWATER THIS PLATE IS MOST RESPECTFULLY INSCRIBED.
Published Aug.t 25, 1827 by Jones & C.o 3 Acton Place, Kingsland Road, London.

The Regent's Canal, London (1820)

The main form of inland transport was either by dirt road or by river. However, Birmingham lacked a large river. Also Birmingham and Stoke needed to have a transport link to major seaports like London and Liverpool. Without good transport links these towns and their industries would find it difficult to grow.

Canals proved to be the answer. These were man-made waterways. The Chinese were the first to build canals at the time when the Romans ruled Britain. The Dutch and French had built canals in the seventeenth century. In the eighteenth century Britain began to develop a canal network. This aimed to join towns that made manufactured goods to seaports and major cities.

By 1815, Britain was criss-crossed with canals. These connected Birmingham with all the major towns and seaports. Birmingham ended up with more miles of canals than Venice!

Canals allowed raw materials to be brought to factories cheaply and in large amounts. The finished goods were then transported away from factories by the same canal. The goods were transported in barges, like the ones in the picture. The barges were pulled by horses. Although transport by canal barge could be slow, travelling at only a few miles an hour, it was much cheaper than transporting goods by road.

Building canals was not easy. Large amounts of water had to be found. So canals had large reservoirs built to provide a constant supply of water.

Joining places at different heights also provided problems. Tunnels and bridges could be built. These were expensive. However, today there are many canals still used which have tunnels and bridges. An important way to solve the problem was to build locks. A lock contained a chamber where barges could enter and the water level could be changed up or down, to link canals with different height levels. A lock is shown in the picture.

Canals were the main highways of Britain's industrial revolution until the development of railways. Railways were much faster and could transport heavier loads than canals. By the 1850s canals were in decline.

Now it's your turn

1 Can you identify why Britain needed canals in the eighteenth century?
2 What changes do you think canals brought to Britain in the eighteenth century?
3 What problems faced canal builders and how did they try to overcome them?

Check your progress

☆ I can describe how canals developed and why they were difficult to build.
☆☆ I can explain why canals were built, and who built them.
☆☆☆ I can identify reasons to show why canals were important to the Industrial Revolution.

Great engineers: George Stephenson

Objectives

By the end of this unit you will be able to:

- describe the work of George Stephenson
- assess Stephenson's significance

George Stephenson was a transport engineer, famous for the design and construction of locomotives and railways.

Getting you thinking

Do you know when the railways were first built, and why? Can you think of any new railways that have been built in our own time?

George Stephenson (1781–1848) began his working life as a colliery worker. After attending night school, he worked his way up to become *enginewright* at Killingworth *Colliery* near Newcastle. At this time, he learned about the workings of steam engines, and in 1814 he built his first *locomotive*. Four years later he designed a miner's safety lamp, the Geordie lamp, used by miners in the Newcastle area. This is one possible explanation for the modern term 'Geordie'. But it was as a builder of locomotives and of railways that his reputation was really made.

Between 1822 and 1825, he built the first railway designed for locomotives. This ran from the coal mines at Bishop Auckland through Darlington to the port of Stockton on the River Tees. One of the most important decisions that Stephenson took when building this line was the width of the rails, or gauge. He chose a narrow gauge and this is now the standard width for much of the world's railways today. He also realised that it was important for railway lines to be as level as possible.

The Rocket Locomotive

Enginewright: an engineer in charge of a coal mine
Colliery: a coal mine

The opening of the Liverpool and Manchester Railway in 1830. The local MP, William Huskisson, was killed on the day of the opening.

The success of the Stockton to Darlington line led to Stephenson being appointed chief engineer of the Liverpool and Manchester Railway. Its building required him to solve several engineering problems, the most difficult being the Sankey Viaduct, which carried the railway over the Sankey Brook. He also had to make a cutting through rock and a two kilometre-long tunnel. With his son Robert, he also built the Rocket, the best performing locomotive in the trials held to decide which locomotives would be used on the railway. When it opened in 1830, it was the first passenger railway in the world. One man, the local MP William Huskisson, died in a rail accident on its opening day, but this did nothing to slow the development of the railways. In the 'railway mania' of the 1840s, hundreds of railway companies were set up and thousands of miles of track laid. Eventually, as Stephenson had predicted, these were all joined together, using the same gauge.

People came from all over the world to learn from Stephenson. He became wealthy and was able to marry the first woman he had courted as a young man. Her family had considered him too poor to be a good match at the time. Today he is commemorated by three statues – two outside Newcastle and Chesterfield railway stations, and one at the National Railway Museum in York.

Now it's your turn

Create a cartoon strip telling the story of George Stephenson's life and work. Use the internet to find pictures of Stephenson's inventions which you can copy from, and provide captions in each box to tell the story in words.

Check your progress

★ I can describe the work of George Stephenson.

★★ I can describe how significant he is.

★★★ I can explain how his work is significant to us today.

Locomotive: a steam engine that moves along rails

Great engineers: Brunel

Isambard Kingdom Brunel is another great Victorian engineer, famous for the railways and ships he designed and built.

Getting you thinking

- What does an engineer do? Why do you think some Victorian engineers are so famous?

Isambard Kingdom Brunel (1806–59) was born in England and educated in France. In 1822 he returned to England to assist his father, who was working on a tunnel under the river Thames in London.

At the beginning of the nineteenth century, London was vastly overcrowded. The dockland area was even busier and needed to expand. Engineers decided the best way to connect the north to the south side of the river was underground. This was a difficult engineering challenge and workers faced many problems.

The conditions under the river were dangerous and fatal for many workers. The rotting sewage created a foul smell and caused fever and blindness. Brunel worked for days on end with only short breaks to eat and sleep. In 1827, the tunnel flooded and Brunel had to make a quick escape. The riverbanks burst again in 1828 and several men were killed. As the river washed its way through the tunnel, Brunel was trapped under a large piece of timber. He suffered internal injuries and took six months to recover. He never worked on the Thames tunnel again.

In 1833, Brunel was appointed chief engineer of the Great Western Railway (GWR). Brunel changed the way people could travel by widening the distance between the rails on which trains ran. This, he argued, allowed trains to travel faster, made the journey smoother for passengers, and allowed more *freight* to be carried. Brunel's innovation was used successfully throughout the GWR network from London to Bristol and to Exeter. Despite the success of his innovation in the west country, Brunel's invention was too expensive to maintain. The government decided

Isambard Kingdom Brunel

to impose a standard gauge over the country, and George Stephenson's narrow gauge was favoured. Amongst his engineering achievements Brunel designed the Box Tunnel, the longest railway tunnel in the world at the time.

As part of his railway work Brunel designed and built the Royal Albert Bridge over the River Tamar in Plymouth. He designed the Clifton Suspension Bridge in Bristol, although it was not completed until after his death. He also built steamships. His SS Great Britain, launched in 1843, was the first modern ship, built of iron and driven by a steam engine that turned its propellers. In 1858, the Great Eastern steamship was completed – at the time, the largest ship in the world. The Great Eastern suffered many problems. It was very expensive to produce and its size and weight made it difficult to launch. Brunel believed that a traveller should be able to catch a steam train in London and connect with a steam ship that would cross the Atlantic to New York.

The Great Eastern, 1858

All of Brunel's engineering achievements made him famous at the time, and many of his structures still remain in use today. He is commemorated today by six statues in various places he was associated with, such as Bristol.

Extension work

Study the photograph of the Great Eastern. Can you think of any other problems the ship may have encountered?

Local history

The six statues of Brunel are located in places that he had an effect on. Is there someone historically significant with a connection to your local area? If so what sort of statue would you like to see? Where would you place it?

Now it's your turn

1 Study the photograph of Brunel carefully. Which one of Brunel's achievements would you associate with this picture?
2 Which of Brunel's achievements and inventions do you think was most important at the time?

Check your progress

⭐ I can describe the work of Isambard Kingdom Brunel.

⭐⭐ I can decide how significant he is.

⭐⭐⭐ I can explain why he is significant.

How did the Industrial Revolution change the lives of ordinary people?

An important part of the study of history is looking at change over time. In history there have been periods of rapid change and also periods of stability or little change.

One of the tasks of a historian is to identify and then measure the amount of change. One of the most important changes to how people lived in Britain was the Industrial Revolution. It changed where people lived, how they worked and how much wealth they possessed.

You have been studying how the Industrial Revolution impacted on the lives of ordinary people.

A view of the river Irwell in Manchester in the nineteenth century

Now you are going to carry out a task that will help you to check your progress. Read the instructions very carefully. They tell you what to do. They tell you how to plan your task. They tell you how your work will be assessed.

 ## Assessment task: write and record a talk for radio

You are going to write a one-minute radio talk for young people. It is called 'What did the Industrial Revolution mean for ordinary people's lives?'

Planning

1   Think about the main aspects of working people's lives, their housing, food, health and ability to travel.

2   Thinking about these aspects, study the photo of the river Irwell in Manchester. What does this image tell us about the towns in which ordinary people lived?

3   What elements of the Industrial Revolution are shown in the picture?

4   Note down what you think affected ordinary people's lives and think about how it is shown in the picture.

5   Use your notes to prepare your one-minute talk. Remember that you want to keep it brief but interesting. You might include an historian's comments or the words of someone writing at the time to add interest.

6   After careful rehearsal, record your one-minute talk.

Check your level

I can include at least one person, event or change.

I can describe the impact of that person, event or change.

I can use some historical words.

Level 3

I can include several people, events or changes.

I can clearly describe the impact those people, events and changes made.

I can use historical terms in my talk.

Level 4

I can show knowledge of how the lives of working people were changed.

I can describe those people, events and changes that had the greatest impact.

I can use historical terms to help make my ideas clear.

Level 5

2 Why did people want the vote?

Objectives

By the end of this unit you will know:

- which people wanted the right to vote and why
- how to use sources to find out about the past

Parliamentary election: voting to decide who will be the members of parliament (MPs) who run the country

In 1819, around 60,000 people gathered in St. Peter's Square in Manchester to protest. They wanted the right to vote in *parliamentary elections* and an end to famine. Henry Hunt, a political speaker, led the protest. The local *magistrates* were frightened by the meeting and sent in the troops to arrest Hunt; he was imprisoned for two years. The Peterloo Massacre resulted in the death of eleven people and left 400 injured. The artist has drawn his version of what happened that day.

Questions

1 Describe what this picture shows.
2 Whose side is the artist on? How do you know?
3 Why do you think people were prepared to risk injury or death to demonstrate for the right to vote?

Magistrate: local person responsible for law and order, sometimes known as a Justice of the Peace (JP)

The causes of protest

Look at the picture. It shows a mob burning down a farm in Kent. This took place during the Captain Swing riots. These were some of the most important protests that took place in the early nineteenth century.

Objectives

By the end of this lesson you will be able to:

- describe some events which involved protest
- understand some of the reason why protests took place
- make judgements about why protests took place

Getting you thinking

Throughout the nineteenth and early twentieth centuries people protested for a variety of reasons. Some were hungry and protested for more food. Some disliked industrial change, which they thought would threaten their jobs. Others wanted political power.

Some of the protests were limited to parts of the country. Other protests were countrywide.

Fear of protest was an important reason behind the development of a modern police force. The first police force was formed in Ireland in 1812, then in London in 1829. From 1839, police forces were created across Britain.

A mob burning down a farm in Kent

A century of protests

Protests against the Corn Laws

The biggest part of people's diet in Britain in the early nineteenth century was bread. So the price of bread was very important. In 1815 parliament passed the Corn Laws, which created a high price for grain. This pleased farmers. There were many farmers in parliament.

However, these laws also increased the price of bread. Many farm workers and industrial workers became very angry. Demonstrations against the Corn Laws spread across Britain. In 1816, hundreds of angry farm workers attacked the town of Littleport in Cambridgeshire. Troops had to be used to stop the protests.

Protests against new machinery

The Industrial Revolution brought many changes. The introduction of machines that could do the work of many men led to workers losing their jobs. In an attempt to keep their jobs, some workers tried to destroy machinery. In 1811, a group of industrial workers, called the 'Luddites', destroyed cloth-making machinery in towns such as Nottingham.

During the Captain Swing riots of 1831, farm workers in counties such as Kent destroyed machines that threshed corn to produce seed.

Both these protests were taken very seriously by the government – soldiers were sent to put down the Nottingham protests in 1811. After the Captain Swing riots, the government changed the Poor Law and created workhouses for the unemployed.

Protests for political power

In 1800 very few adults had the right to vote. Most people in parliament were rich landowners. Ordinary people protested. In 1816 and 1819, demonstrations for an increase in the number who could vote were broken up by soldiers. A number of people died as a result of the 1819 demonstration in Manchester, so it was given the name Peterloo, after the Battle of Waterloo.

The biggest movement for more political power took place in the years 1836 to 1850. This was called the Chartist movement. Hundreds of thousands of people joined the call for political power to be given to ordinary people. Many who protested feared they would lose their jobs to new machinery.

Now it's your turn

1 Identify two reasons why people protested.
2 What links can you make between the reasons why people protested?

Check your progress

I can describe events that led to protests.
I can explain why protests took place.
I can give reasons why people protested and why police forces were established.

47

Why did people want a vote in parliamentary elections?

Today, as in the 1830s, this country is run by parliament, but who is able to vote in elections has changed.

Getting you thinking

Look at the cartoon. It depicts John Bull who was a symbol of Britain.

- Do you think the cartoonist thought voting reform would be good for Britain?

Before 1832, only 3 percent of Britain's population could vote. The right to vote depended on how wealthy you were; this included how much you earned and the value of your property. This meant that women and poor people could not vote. Voters had to live in particular areas and own certain types of property. In the boxes on the right are some of the different ways that the country was divided.

In this cartoon, the legendary figure of John Bull (representing Britain) looks forward to what voting reform might bring

Borough: an area that sends MPs to parliament

County constituencies

All men who owned property worth 40 shillings a year could vote. In the *boroughs*, it depended what type of borough it was.

Burgage boroughs

The votes belonged to the male owners of particular properties or 'burgage' plots. None of these boroughs had more than 400 voters. Most had less than 200. In the worst example, Old Sarum, just seven voters elected the two members of parliament (MPs).

Potwalloper boroughs

The votes belonged to any man who owned a property with a fireplace and lockable door. You proved this by rattling your key in your cooking pot – potwalloping! Nearly half of these boroughs had 200 or fewer voters.

Scot and lot boroughs

The votes belonged to those men who paid local taxes. Some of these boroughs had many voters but others had 200 or fewer voters. In the worst example, Gatton, the owners of six houses elected the two MPs.

In 1832, parliament passed the Reform Act. Before the act, the electoral system had not changed much since the 1600s. The Industrial Revolution saw towns grow vastly; this meant more people in certain areas needed to be heard by parliament. The Reform Act allowed growing industrial towns greater representation in parliament than the sparsely populated and wealthy rural areas.

The abolition of these voting rules did allow more people to vote but voters still had to own expensive property. This excluded poorer people. There were still many people who wanted greater reform of the electoral system, and who wanted more people like themselves to be allowed to vote. If you wanted improvements in your living conditions you needed someone to represent your concerns in parliament. Wealthy and poor people had different concerns so were more than likely to vote for different people. Without the right to vote, people could not get parliament to make positive changes to their lives.

- Think about a time when you have needed help. You may have found it unfair if others received help and you did not. How did that make you feel? Poorer people felt that the government was not helping them, despite the changes made by the Reform Act. They found it difficult to explain this without the ability to vote. How do you think not being able to vote affected these people?

Now it's your turn

Parliament was made up of roughly 650 MPs who represented a constituency. There were two types of constituency, county and borough. Each usually had two MPs.

1 Decide who could vote for those MPs and who could not, using the examples of different kinds of constituency in the box above.

2 What problems do you think these small numbers of voters would cause?

Check your progress

I can describe who could vote before the Reform Act.

I can explain why voting was important.

I can explain some of the effects of the Reform Act.

How did the Chartists campaign for the vote?

Objectives

By the end of this lesson you will be able to:

- describe what the Chartists wanted
- explain how they tried to achieve their aims

After the 1832 Reform Act, working men and those without much property were still not able to vote. The Chartists were a group of working men who campaigned to be allowed to vote. Let's find out how they went about it.

Getting you thinking

One of the groups who did not own property, and so could not vote in elections, were ordinary working men. They wanted changes made to their lives. They worked long hours in the new factories and often lived in very poor conditions in the new factory towns. If they lost their jobs, the only options were to starve or go into a workhouse. They wanted parliament to pass laws to improve their lives, but realised that this would not happen until they had the vote. So they organised a protest movement, which became known as Chartism. This name came from the People's Charter, which had a six-point list of demands:

- A vote for every man over the age of 21
- Votes to be cast in secret
- MPs should not have to own property
- MPs should be paid
- Each constituency should have an equal number of voters
- Elections should be held every year

The Chartists campaigned by organising petitions, on three occasions: in 1839, 1842 and 1848. They published a newspaper called the *Northern Star*, held meetings and demonstrations and went on strike. In November 1839, the Chartists armed themselves and tried to capture Newport, this became known as the Newport Rising. The battle lasted only half an hour.

The government did not listen to the Chartists. Many of their leaders and members were arrested. Some were fined or imprisoned and others transported to Australia. The movement disappeared after 1848, partly because of the government's actions and partly because living and working conditions improved. Many former Chartists turned their attention to other causes, such as education and the cooperative movement.

Street mural in Newport, South Wales commemorating the Newport Rising in 1839

Now it's your turn

1   There were reasons for each of the six points in the People's Charter. Can you match each reason with the relevant point in the Charter?

   Reasons:
   - Any man could be an MP.
   - Everyone's vote would have equal value and there would be no small constituencies where the vote could be fixed.
   - Working men could afford to become MPs.
   - No voter could be bribed or intimidated, as no one would know how they had voted.
   - The MPs in parliament would have to do what the voters wanted them to do, otherwise they could be voted out.
   - Working men would be able to vote.

2   The Chartists campaigned for the vote in a variety of ways. Read the list of actions they took, and try to place them into two different categories. Clue: There were Chartists who were known as 'Moral Force' Chartists, and others who were known as 'Physical Force' Chartists. What do you think these phrases mean?

Extension work

Which of the six points of the People's Charter have now been met?

Check your progress

★   I can describe who could not vote after the 1832 Reform Act.

★★   I can explain why the Chartists wanted the six points of the People's Charter.

★★★   I can explain how the Chartists campaigned.

How did women campaign for the vote?

Objectives

By the end of this lesson you will be able to:

- describe why women wanted the vote
- explain how they tried to achieve their aims

It was not just working men who wanted the vote; women wanted the vote too.

Getting you thinking

The photograph below shows suffragettes on their release from prison in 1908, parading through the streets of London on an open-top vehicle. They had been sent to prison for campaigning for the vote. So why did women want the vote?

The 1832 Reform Act allowed more men to vote, and some women wanted the vote too. This demand increased after 1867 when all men over the age of 21 gained the *suffrage*. Some women saw having the vote as an essential step towards equality in all aspects of life, such as education, work and the family.

The first women's suffrage societies were formed in the 1850s. They joined together into the National Union of Women's Suffrage Societies (NUWSS) led by Millicent Fawcett. They were called *Suffragists*. Some MPs agreed with them, but still women were not given the vote. Frustrated by this lack of progress, Emmeline Pankhurst set up a new society, the Women's Social and Political Union (WSPU) in 1903. Only women could join and thousands did, both rich and poor. They became known as the *Suffragettes*.

Source 1 *Suffragettes parading after their release from prison, 1908*

Suffrage: the right to vote
Suffragist: peaceful campaigner for women's right to vote

The Suffragists campaigned by:

- writing letters to MPs and newspapers
- organising petitions
- printing leaflets
- holding meetings and marches

The Suffragettes first campaigned by:

- chaining themselves to railings
- making banners
- going on processions
- chalking slogans on pavements
- creating photographic opportunities such as the bus parade
- publishing a newspaper, *Votes for Women*

After 1910 the Suffragettes campaigned by:

- smashing windows and street lamps
- setting fire to post boxes
- arson attacks on houses, churches and racecourse stands
- slashing paintings in galleries
- cutting telephone wires
- sabotaging greens on golf courses
- planting bombs in London, Doncaster and Dublin

Source 3
Emmeline Pankhurst is arrested

'The argument of the broken window pane is the most valuable argument in modern politics.'

'Deeds not words.'

'There is something that Governments care for far more than human life, and that is the security of property, and so it is through property that we shall strike the enemy.'

Source 2 *Emmeline Pankhurst*

Now it's your turn APP

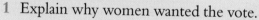

1 Explain why women wanted the vote.
2 Why do you think, if some MPs listened to the Suffragists and supported their campaign, did they still not get the right to vote?
3 Read the quotes from Emmeline Pankhurst in Source 1. Do you think she was in favour of the more violent campaigning methods adopted by the Suffragettes after 1910?
4 If she saw the photograph of herself (Source 2) in a newspaper, what might her reaction have been?

Extension work

How were the methods of the Suffragettes similar to and different from those of the Chartists?

Check your progress

I can describe why women wanted the vote.
I can describe some of the tactics they used.
I can explain why some used peaceful protest and others used violence.

Suffragette: militant (more extreme) campaigner for women's right to vote

When and why were changes made to the vote, 1832–1928?

Objectives

By the end of this lesson you will be able to:

- use a timeline to explore changes to the vote
- describe how voting rights were increased
- explain some of the reasons for this and its consequences

The campaigns of the Chartists, the Suffragists and the Suffragettes show that the right to vote was considered very important.

Getting you thinking

The Reform Act of 1832 was for many people only the start of the campaign for suffrage expansion. Although it gave voting rights to some wealthy men, the number of people able to vote was still limited.

As you know, the Chartists began campaigning for suffrage soon after the passing of the Reform Act that excluded them from voting. It took nearly 30 years before 'respectable' working men gained the vote in 1867. There remained a large number of working class men who still could not vote. Similarly, the women's suffrage movement started in 1850 and it was another 78 years before women could vote – and even then, not all women were included. What eventually persuaded governments to change voting rights?

The timeline on the right allows us to compare events and when they happened. Thinking back to what you have learnt about voting reform, can you see any patterns between campaigns for voting rights and changes to voting rights?

'The March of the Women', a suffragette song sheet

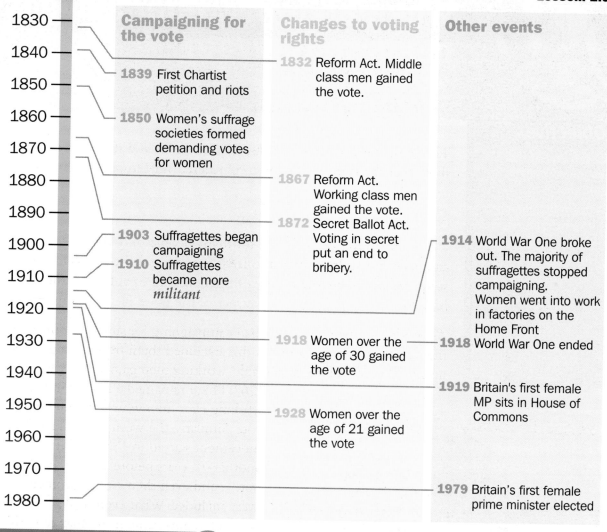

	Campaigning for the vote	Changes to voting rights	Other events
1830			
1840		**1832** Reform Act. Middle class men gained the vote.	
1850	**1839** First Chartist petition and riots		
1860	**1850** Women's suffrage societies formed demanding votes for women		
1870			
1880		**1867** Reform Act. Working class men gained the vote.	
1890		**1872** Secret Ballot Act. Voting in secret put an end to bribery.	
1900	**1903** Suffragettes began campaigning		
1910	**1910** Suffragettes became more *militant*		**1914** World War One broke out. The majority of suffragettes stopped campaigning. Women went into work in factories on the Home Front
1920			
1930		**1918** Women over the age of 30 gained the vote	**1918** World War One ended
1940			**1919** Britain's first female MP sits in House of Commons
1950		**1928** Women over the age of 21 gained the vote	
1960			
1970			
1980			**1979** Britain's first female prime minister elected

Now it's your turn   APP

Think about the strategies used by the Chartists, the Suffragists, and the Suffragettes in their campaigns. Some used violent forms of protest, others used peaceful means of protest. Compare when and how the groups protested with other events on the timeline. Then try and answer these questions:

1 Did the campaigning by the Chartists lead to working class men gaining the vote?
2 How effective were the violent tactics of the Chartists and the Suffragettes?
3 Was the campaigning of the Suffragettes the most important reason why women gained the vote? Can you think of any other reasons?
4 What other connections can you make between the events in the timeline?
5 Are there other events which should be included in this story?

Check your progress

★ I can describe some connections between events.

★★ I can explain how events are connected.

★★★ I can use a timeline to show how events are connected.

Militant: using extreme tactics in support of a cause

Why was a new Poor Law needed?

Objectives

By the end of this lesson you will be able to:

- describe some of the reasons why the Poor Law was passed
- explain which reasons were most important

Today the government provides welfare for people in need, particularly those suffering from ill health. But this was not always the case.

Getting you thinking

In the reign of Elizabeth I, the 1605 Poor Law made each *parish* responsible for its poor people. Property owners paid a *poor rate*, which was collected by the overseer of the poor. He used this money to look after poor people. In some parishes there was a workhouse where the poor went to live, but in most they stayed in their own homes and were given money for food and rent. This was known as outdoor relief.

There were two types of poor, those who were seen as being poor through no fault of their own – the sick, disabled, elderly, orphaned and widowed; and the 'able-bodied' poor – those who were capable of work but who were unemployed. The overseer and rate-payers were keen to find work for the able-bodied poor to keep the costs down.

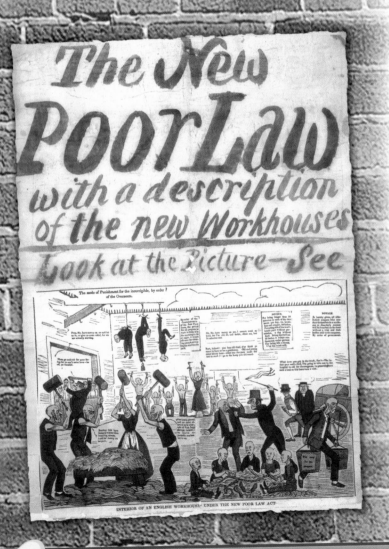

A poster protesting against the Poor Law

Parish: the area around a church
Poor rate: a local tax

This system worked up until the rapid changes of the Industrial Revolution. From about 1815 onwards, there were five main reasons why the system struggled, leading some people to call for change.

1. Attitudes to the poor

Some argued that the payment of outdoor relief encouraged the poor to be idle and to have large families. Others accused the overseers of being incompetent. Some workhouses were criticised for being too comfortable.

2. Growth of towns

When the parish was just the people of a village or an area of a small town, it was quite straightforward to manage the Poor Law system. But as the new towns and cities grew so quickly, they swamped the system. There were just too many people and problems for a single overseer to manage.

3. Changes in the countryside

Changes in farming, a series of poor harvests and high food prices all led to more people claiming *poor relief* in the countryside.

4. Changes in industry

The industrial changes led to large numbers of people working in the same trade in an area. When trade was poor, thousands could be thrown out of work at the same time, swamping the poor relief system.

5. Costs

Costs rose from roughly £4 million a year in 1803 to over £7 million in 1832.

Now it's your turn

Study the reasons carefully.
1 Which are connected?
2 Which do you think might have worried people most at the time? Why?

In 1832 a Royal Commission was set up to investigate the problem. It concluded that a new Poor Law was required. This was passed in 1834. It set up a new system. Parishes were combined into unions and each Poor Law union built a workhouse. To receive help, the poor would have to go and live in the workhouse.

Check your progress

☆   I can describe one reason why the Elizabethan Poor Law fell short of what was needed.

☆☆   I can show how changes in society created the need for a new Poor Law.

☆☆☆   I can suggest why people thought the 1834 Poor Law might solve the problem of extreme poverty.

Poor relief: money given to help the poor

What was life like in the workhouse?

Objectives

By the end of this lesson you will be able to:

- use sources to answer an historical question
- describe what life was like in the workhouse
- explain how the workhouse was made 'less eligible'

Getting you thinking

Under the 1834 Poor Law Act, each Poor Law union was run by a board of guardians. They replaced the old overseers. It was they who built and ran the workhouses. The Poor Law had two underlying principles. One was that the poor should be treated the same no matter where they lived. The second was 'less eligibility'. This meant that life in the workhouse should be made harder than the life of the worst-off labourer living outside it, so that the poor would only go into the workhouse as a last resort.

1 Twelve single Beds.

2 First class, 30 in double Beds.

3 Closet.

4 First class, 38 in single Beds, in two tiers.

5 Twelve single Beds.

6 Thirty-six in single Beds, in two tiers.

7 Clerk.

8 Strong Room.

9 Anti-Room.

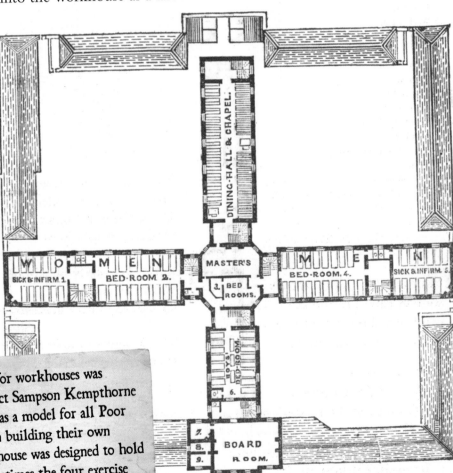

First floor of a workhouse

The square plan design for workhouses was produced by the architect Sampson Kempthorne in 1835. It was produced as a model for all Poor Law unions to use when building their own workhouses. The workhouse was designed to hold 300 to 500 people. Sometimes the four exercise yards were divided into smaller separate areas.

Source 1

1 Work Room.
2 Store.
3 Receiving Wards, 3 beds.
4 Bath.
5 Washing Room.
6 Receiving Ward, 3 beds.
7 Washing Room.
8 Work Room.
9 Flour and Mill Room.
10 Coals.
11 Bakehouse.
12 Bread Room.
13 Searching Room.
14 Porter's Room.
15 Store.
16 Potatoes.
17 Coals.
18 Work Room.
19 Washing Room.
20 Receiving Ward, 3 beds.
21 Washing Room.
22 Bath.
23 Receiving Ward, 3 beds.
24 Laundry.
25 Wash-house.
26 Dead House.
27 Refractory Ward.
28 Work Room.
29 Piggery.
30 Slaughter House.
31 Work Room.
32 Refractory Ward.
33 Dead House.
34 Women's Stairs to Dining Hall.
35 Men's Stairs to ditto.
36 Boys' and Girls' School and Dining Room.
37 Delivery.
38 Passage.
39 Well.
40 Cellar under ground.

Ground floor of a workhouse

Now it's your turn

Your task is to study these two sources carefully and see what you can learn about how the poor were treated in the workhouse.

Hints for Source 1
- What did the doors and windows of the master's room look over?
- What do you think might have been the purpose of the searching room, the receiving ward and the *refractory* ward?
- What were the main food items?

Any Pauper, being an inmate of the Workhouse, who shall make any noise when silence is ordered to be kept;
Or shall refuse or neglect to work
Or shall pretend sickness
                    Shall be deemed DISORDERLY.
Any Pauper who Shall unlawfully strike any person;
Or shall be drunk;
Or shall act or write indecently or obscenely
                    Shall be deemed REFRACTORY.
The Guardian may order any refractory pauper to be punished by confinement in a separate room.

Source 2 *Toxteth Park workhouse rules*

Check your progress

I can describe life in the workhouse.
I can use sources to test the idea that life in the workhouse was unpleasant.
I can explain why life was made hard for workhouse inmates.

Law and order: the police

Law and order was another problem in the growing towns. The increasing population of urban areas led to higher rates of crime and violence. A solution was needed to control and protect people from criminal behaviour.

Getting you thinking

In the eighteenth century, law and order was the responsibility of parish constables and nightwatchmen. These were part-time, poorly paid, few in number and often of poor quality. Watchmen were nicknamed 'Charleys'. They could not keep law and order in the growing towns and cities. This problem was most obvious in London.

In 1750 the *magistrate* Henry Fielding set up the Bow Street Runners, made up of seven constables based in his London office. Their job was to track down criminals. They were an early type of police, but they did not patrol the streets or attempt to prevent crime.

Members of Robert Peel's Irish police force

Magistrate: local person who administers the law and deals with minor crimes

In 1798, merchants trading with the West Indies clubbed together to fund a river police force, based at Wapping. They were losing money because of thefts from their ships in London's docks. They employed 220 men who did not wear uniforms but carried weapons. This was the first police force whose presence acted as a deterrent to crime. In their first year, over 2,000 people who were arrested were found guilty of offences. The force was so successful that it was taken over by the government in 1801.

This success also encouraged another magistrate, Richard Ford, to set up the Bow Street horse patrol in 1805. They were intended to stop highwaymen from robbing travellers. The 54 men were the first uniformed policemen. They wore blue coats and scarlet waistcoats and were nicknamed 'Robin Redbreasts'.

In 1828 the *home secretary* Sir Robert Peel convinced MPs to pass an act of parliament which set up the Metropolitan Police Force. It employed 2,880 uniformed men, armed with truncheons, to patrol the streets.

Read Source 1. How many facts can you identify? How many judgements?

'It was in 1829 that Peel established the Metropolitan Police Force for London based at Scotland Yard. The 1,000 constables employed were affectionately nicknamed 'Bobbies' or, somewhat less affectionately, 'Peelers' (both terms are still used today). Although unpopular at first they proved very successful in cutting crime in London, and by 1857 all cities in the UK were obliged to form their own police forces. Known as the father of modern policing, Robert Peel...

Source 1 *from A.Ramsay, Sir Robert Peel, 1969*

Now it's your turn

Source 1 is an historical interpretation. By describing Peel as 'the father of modern policing', it is giving him the credit for starting the first police force.

Your task is to look at the development of the police, to examine the role of Peel and others, and decide if you agree with this interpretation.
- Should the police be nicknamed 'Henrys'?
- Should Richard Ford be described as 'the father of modern policing'?
- Details you might consider are: numbers, uniform, weapons, role

Check your progress

I can describe the early types of police.
I can explain why Peel might called 'the father of modern policing'.
I can explain why others might also be given this name.

Law and order: the Victorian prison

Objectives

By the end of this lesson you will be able to:

- describe aspects of life in a reformed prison
- explain why prisoners were treated this way

Pentonville was built in 1842 as a model prison. It is still in use today, but the way prisoners are treated has changed.

Getting you thinking

The nineteenth-century reformers who had been concerned with living and working conditions for ordinary people also wanted improvements in prisons. They campaigned for clean drinking water, clean living conditions, a doctor in each prison and food provided for prisoners instead of them having to buy their own. The reformers also wanted to stop prisoners from mixing. They felt this led to more crime as criminals learned from each other. They wanted prisoners to do useful rather than pointless work.

Source 1 *Convicts exercising in Pentonville prison, an illustration from Mayhew & Binny's 'The Criminal Prisons of London', 1862*

The Model Prison, intended to form the standard upon which our county gaols are hereafter to be erected, … consists of five divisions of three stories each, radiating from a common centre, and subdivided into cells that are calculated to contain 520 prisoners. It is formed in furtherance of the separate and silent system, which, as here carried out, prevents the possibility of contact between the wretched inmates, who, confined in solitary cells, and exercised singly between bare walls … are never permitted to see each other.

Source 2 *from Mogg's 'New Picture of London and Visitor's Guide to its Sights', 1844.*

Source 4 *An aerial view of Strangeways prison in Manchester, built on the same design as Pentonville*

The food is very fair both as to quantity and quality. You get beef and mutton on alternate days, with enough bread and vegetables; and cocoa for breakfast and gruel for supper. The labour is performed in the privacy of your own cell, and if you don't know a trade they teach you one. They taught me shoemaking. ... if I may be permitted to express an opinion on the subject, I may say that I consider it a great advantage and privilege to be allowed to work when in prison at some trade free men work at. It saves you from sinking as low in your value of yourself as when you are set at spending an entire day at tearing a lot of tarred rope in pieces ['picking oakum'], all the while knowing that a machine would do the work in five minutes or less.

You get a clean shirt and stockings and neckerchief once a week, and a clean flannel shirt and drawers once a fortnight. A bath once a fortnight. For exercise you are allowed to tramp round a circle made of paving stones in the yard.

Source 3 *A description of his time in Pentonville, taken from James Greenwood's 'The Wilds of London', 1874.*

Now it's your turn

1 Study source 1. Can you explain why they are wearing masks and holding a rope?
2 What 'improvements' to prison life are described in sources 2 and 3?
3 What might be the effect of these improvements?

Check your progress

⭐ I can describe what Pentonville was like.
⭐⭐ I can explain what changes were made to prison life in the nineteenth century.
⭐⭐⭐ I can suggest what the effect of these improvements might have been.

How did the Victorians clean up their towns and cities?

Objectives

By the end of this lesson you will be able to:

- describe the social improvements needed in urban areas
- explain what caused local governments to take action

During the Industrial Revolution, the population of urban areas grew enormously. This had a great impact on the levels of hygiene in towns and cities.

Getting you thinking

By the middle of the nineteenth century, half of Britain's population lived in towns, where poor hygiene and ineffective sewer systems resulted in the spread of deadly diseases such as cholera and typhoid. In the 1830s, life expectancy in towns was just 29 years.

Before 1835, around 250 towns had received a Royal Charter, allowing them to have their own council. Many expanding towns had not received a Royal Charter and so did not have a council to protect its population. By the 1830s, there was growing criticism of how towns were run. They were accused of corruption as members would vote for their friends and relatives to be on the council and ignore the needs of the townspeople. The government set up a Royal Commission in 1833 to investigate how councils dealt with important functions like water supplies, drainage and street cleaning. The report found that many councils neglected issues of hygiene.

In 1835, parliament took action and the Municipal Corporations Act was passed. The act established boroughs; these were governed by a council and elected by ratepayers. Citizens of these boroughs paid taxes to improve the community in which they lived. However, many councils did not use ratepayers' money for social improvements. In fact, many towns did not have a council and so the needs of its people could not be met. The Reform Act of 1832 did not allow working class men the vote; this meant their needs were neglected too. As a result many cities remained dirty and threatened populations with disease.

Rebuilding the sewers in Fleet Street, London, 1845

In London, wealthy households began using water closets that flushed waste down sewers made originally for carrying rainwater to the Thames. The river became an open sewer. This was then extracted by water companies and sold to customers to drink.

The Great Stink

In the summer of 1858, the smell of sewage in central London was overwhelming. Waste flowed slowly by Westminster and members of parliament were so appalled by the stench that a law to provide more money for sewage systems was passed in just 18 days.

The Great Stink is an example of the way problems can be solved if there is a government or local council with the will to fix it. Can you think of any examples where your local government has solved problems?

Now it's your turn

Look at these two sources. What do you think they suggest about the hygiene of London at this time?

Why do you think it was necessary for local government to reform?

He who drinks a tumbler of London water has literally in his stomach more animated beings than there are men, women and children on the face of the globe ...

Source 1 *Sydney Smith, London resident writing in 1834*

FARADAY GIVING HIS CARD TO FATHER THAMES;
AND WE HOPE THE DIRTY FELLOW WILL CONSULT THE LEARNED PROFESSOR.

Source 2 *Punch 1858, the famous scientist Michael Faraday 'giving his card to Father Thames'*

Check your progress

I can describe how local councils were formed.
I can explain what local councils did to help improve urban areas.
I can explain how poor hygiene prompted local governments to take action.

Welfare reforms

Today we live in a country with a welfare state. This means all the people have free education, free health care and help in old age. This was not the case in Britain before 1900.

Objectives

At the end of the lesson you will be able to:

- explain why welfare reforms were introduced by the Liberal government

Soup kitchen in Manchester, 1862

Preparing the soup

The distribution

Getting you thinking

Look at the pictures above. They show a soup kitchen in the city of Manchester in 1862. At that time there was no government help if you were hungry, sick, got injured at work or were not working. People had to pay for their own welfare. Many people were too poor to pay for their own welfare. The only help offered was in the workhouse (See pp. 58–59).

Many people tried to help the poor. Wealthy people such as Octavia Hill organised housing schemes for the poor. However, no one knew how many people were poor in Britain until the 1880s and 1890s. In 1889 Charles Booth made a detailed study of life in the East End of London. He found very high levels of poverty and ill health. In 1900 Benjamin Seebohm Rowntree, the sweet manufacturer, wrote a study of the city of York. He described the terrible living conditions of almost one quarter of the city's population. Something needed to be done to help the poor.

A major shock to the government came with the South African War of 1899–1902. Thousands of men volunteered to fight, but in cities like London, Liverpool and Glasgow many were rejected because of ill health. If Britain wanted to keep its large empire, it needed strong, fit troops and sailors.

In 1905 the Liberal Party formed a new government. In the period 1905–14 they introduced many reforms that made life easier for the poor and needy.

Liberal welfare reforms

1906 Free school meals for children

1906 Free medical inspection of schoolchildren

1908 Old age pensions

1911 Government help for workers who were sick

1911 Government help for workers who were unemployed

Now it's your turn

1 Look at the reforms in the box above. Which reforms helped Britain get stronger, fitter soldiers and sailors? Give reasons for your answer.
2 How do you think the reforms in 1911 helped make life easier for working people?
3 You are a supporter of the Liberal government's reforms. Produce a poster showing why you think the reforms were important.

Extension work

What support do people today receive from the government to help them with:
- education
- health
- housing
- old age
- unemployment

How does this differ from the help people received from the government by 1914?

Check your progress

I can describe why welfare reforms were introduced.
I can explain why the reforms were important.
I can explain how the reforms affected different groups of people.

Welfare reforms: old age pensions

Objectives

At the end of the lesson you will be able to:

- describe how pensions were introduced
- explain why old age pensions were an important reform

Today, elderly people receive a *pension* from the government, and other help such as payment for heating in very cold weather. In 1900, if you were old and poor you did not receive any support.

Getting you thinking

Look at the picture below. It shows a very important event. On 1 January 1909, elderly people received a weekly pension from the government for the first time. The image shows elderly people at a post office receiving their first pension.

During the nineteenth century many people in Britain had asked the government to introduce a weekly government pension for everyone. Germany had introduced old age pensions in 1889 and this was seen as very successful. If you were poor when you left work, you had to look after yourself or rely on the aid and support of your children. Many elderly people lived with their children and grandchildren.

The only help elderly people received from the government was to go to a workhouse. These were places where facilities were very simple. The elderly were forced to eat and sleep together in large rooms.

The first payment of the weekly pension

Pension: *a sum of money paid to a person who has retired from work*
Convicted: found guilty in a court of law

From 1 January 1909, elderly people over 70 years old received a weekly pension of 5 shillings (25p). This would be the same as £20 today. A married couple received 7 shillings and sixpence (37 pence). These pensions were aimed at the poor because they were for people with incomes of less than 12 shillings per week (60 pence).

Pensions were not given to those who had worked in a workhouse. Also pensions were denied to those who spent long periods without work or who had been *convicted* in a court for drunkenness. Only the 'deserving' poor would receive government support.

The person most responsible for introducing old ages pensions was David Lloyd George, a senior member of the Liberal government.

Although only 500,000 people received pensions, it cost the government 16 million pounds per year. To pay for pensions the government had to increase taxes.

STATE PENSIONS (1908)

- 500,000 pensioners
- Full pension 5 shillings per week, equivalent to £19.30p now
- 1 in 200 lived to age 100
- 10 workers for every pensioner
- 1.2 million aged over 70 (in 1901)

STATE PENSIONS (2008)

- 12 million pensioners
- Full single pension £90.70 per week.
- 1 in 4 will live to age 100
- 4 workers for every pensioner
- 7.2 million aged over 70

Source *Department for Work and Pensions (DWP)*

Now it's your turn

Imagine you are 70 years old on 1 January 1909. You come from a very poor background and have very little money of your own. Write an entry in your diary, describing what you did on that day and how you felt.

Check your progress

I can say when pensions were first introduced.

I can explain reasons why pensions were brought in, and who benefited.

I can explain why the introduction of pensions was a significant historical event.

The impact of the Liberal welfare reforms

Objectives

At the end of the lesson you will be able to:

- describe how the Liberal welfare reforms affected Britain
- explain some of the consequences of the Liberal welfare reform up to 1914

The Liberal welfare reforms of 1905–14 were important in British history. For the first time national government began directly helping the poor, sick, unemployed and elderly.

Getting you thinking

Look at the cartoon. It shows David Lloyd George, who was the chancellor of the exchequer. This was one of the most important jobs in the government. He was responsible for many of the welfare reforms passed by the Liberal government from 1905 to 1914. Many people were unhappy with his decision to tax domestic servants.

Compare the two drawings of Lloyd George: What does the cartoon show us about attitudes towards the Old Age Pension Act?

The welfare reforms made many changes in Britain.

Free school meals

Breakfast every day consisted of porridge with milk and treacle, followed by bread and margarine with milk to drink. At the first breakfast 13 children refused to eat it. At the second breakfast only two refused. From that day on it was liked and enjoyed by all.

Many of the children came from the poorest part of Bradford. Every effort was made to make the meals educational. There were tablecloths and flowers on the table. Some children were monitors. Their job was to lay the tables and serve the other children. From the very start there was little to complain about. The children responded very well to orderly and decent surroundings.

But at the end of the week the tablecloths were very dirty. This was because there was no water at the school for the children to clean their hands.

POLITICAL CIRCUMSTANCES OFTEN ALTER CASES.

Mr LLOYD GEORGE after the OLD AGE PENSION ACT was passed.

Mr LLOYD GEORGE during the passing of the SERVANT TAX

Source 1 *David Lloyd George cartoon from Daily Mirror, 4 December 1912 by WK Hasleden*

Source 2 *From the City of Bradford Education Committee Report in 1907 (From www.nationalarchives.gov.uk)*

National Insurance

The Liberal welfare reforms brought important changes to Britain. Children were better fed. Free medical inspection meant that diseases could be identified at an early stage, preventing future illness. Old age pensions gave elderly poor people a chance to live on their own. National insurance gave workers help when they were sick or unemployed.

By 1914, the Liberal welfare reforms greatly helped people and improved the quality of their lives.

After 1914, other governments introduced more welfare reforms, such as the free National Health Service in 1948.

Source 3 *A Liberal poster of 1911 on the impact of national insurance*

Now it's your turn

1 Study Source 1.
   Describe what is happening in the cartoon.
   Do you think everyone in Britain was a supporter of the reforms?
2 Study Source 2.
   a Describe what breakfast was like for schoolchildren after 1906.
   b Do you think free school meals were a success?
3 Study Source 3.
   a Describe what is happening in the cartoon.
   b What point do you think it is trying to make about the effect of national insurance?

Check your progress

I can describe some reasons why welfare reforms were introduced.
I can explain some of the consequences of the welfare reforms.
I can explain why the reforms were a significant change in Britain.

The changing role of government

Objectives

At the end of the lesson you will be able to:

- describe the changing role of government
- explain how far change took place

From the moment we are born to the time of our death, the government plays an important role in our lives. During the nineteenth and early twentieth centuries, the role of government changed a great deal.

Getting you thinking

Look at the photographs, which show four child convicts in the late nineteenth century.

- What can you learn about them from the pictures and the captions?
- What does this information tell you about Victorian attitudes to children, and to crime?

People thought the government had the role of keeping law and order, so that they could feel safe and free from the fear of crime. Life in a Victorian prison was very harsh – It was meant to be! (See pp. 62–63) Prisons were places where people were punished for committing crimes. Those who committed very serious crimes, such as murder, were executed.

Throughout the nineteenth and early twentieth centuries, everyone regarded this role of government as very important. To help maintain law and order, the government created a police force in London in 1829. Shortly afterwards the whole country was patrolled by police.

Another role of government was to help reduce the number of people who were unemployed. For most of the nineteenth and early twentieth centuries, this was done through the Poor Law (See pp. 58–59). When people became unemployed or were not able to look after themselves, they were forced to live in a workhouse. Life was so harsh that only the desperate and very poor would live there.

A

Date: 1871

Name: Martha Herbert

Age: 12

Punishment: 42 days for stealing £1-12-6d

B
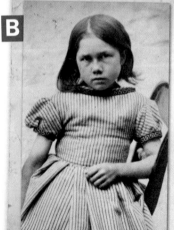
Date: 1870

Name: Julia Ann Crumpling

Age: 7

Punishment: seven days hard labour for stealing a pram

Not all laws passed by Victorian governments were so harsh – some did bring real improvements to people's lives. During the nineteenth century, the government began introducing laws on how factories should run. The maximum hours a person could work was set by the government. The employment of children and women was also limited. By 1914, every factory and business was regulated by laws.

Perhaps, the biggest change to people's everyday lives came from the new powers of local government. Towns, and then the countryside, received the right to choose their own local councils. Many of these councils brought big changes to people's lives. In towns, public parks were created, local transport was organised and clean water introduced. In Birmingham in the 1870s, the city mayor, Joseph Chamberlain, knocked down slum housing and built modern clean housing for the poor. He brought gas and a sewage disposal system to the city. These changes transformed the quality of people's lives.

By 1914, the national government had become directly involved in people's lives. There was a free education system: all children, no matter how poor, could go to school until the age of 13. Children also received free school meals. The elderly received a government pension for the first time. Workers received government help when they were sick or unemployed.

C

Date: 1870

Name: James Hall

Age: 20

Punishment: 42 days for stealing two boxes

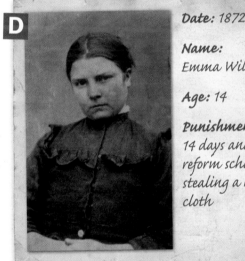

D

Date: 1872

Name: Emma Wilks

Age: 14

Punishment: 14 days and reform school for stealing a neck cloth

Now it's your turn

Give a five-minute classroom talk on the changing role of government in Britain in the nineteenth and early twentieth centuries. You will need to show:
- where the role of government remained the same
- where the role of government changed

Give reasons where and why you think the role of government increased.

Check your progress

★ I can describe some of the changes in ordinary life in the nineteenth and early twentieth centuries.

★★ I can explain the role of local government in bringing about these changes.

★★★ I can describe how the role of government changed over this period.

Why do people have different views on historical events?

Women having dinner in a workhouse, about 1900

History is about studying the past. Historians study evidence from which they make an assessment, or interpretation, of the past.

In unit 2 you have covered the topic of protest and reform. This has involved studying how Britain changed from 1800 to World War One, which began in 1914. During this period Britain went through major changes. There were changes in how Britain was governed and who had the right to decide who was in the government. There were also major changes in how Britain treated poor and vulnerable people.

When studying this period, people have had different views on why events took place, whether or not they were important and how effective they were. As you have discovered, some people believe the Chartists and the Suffragettes were too violent, others disagree. Who is right? Well, both are! It depends on how you interpret the past.

 ## Assessment task: create a TV programme

You are going to show how much you understand about the changes that occurred as a result of reform, by creating a short television programme. Choose a topic related to social reform and assess its successes and failures. Here are some suggestions:

- conditions in reformed Victorian prisons
- condition in the workhouses
- Victorian sewers
- old age pension reform

1 Choose a topic that you think will interest your viewers.
2 Write a short script that introduces your topic. Clearly explain what you think are its successes and its failures.
3 Support your opinions with evidence; these may be written sources or facts that you have discovered.
4 You will need to find images to help you explain your point and make it interesting for people to watch.
5 After careful practice, 'create' your television programme, using help from classmates to display your images, and maybe act out short scenes in character.

Check your level

I can introduce and talk about a reform. I can name at least one success and one failure of a reform. I can use some historical words.	I can describe the successes and failures of a reform. I can clearly describe the impact these successes and failures had on people's lives. I can use historical terms in my television script.	I can show knowledge of how social reform affected the lives of people. I can select and explain how successful or unsuccessful aspects of a certain reform were, and give reasons. I can use historical images to make my ideas clear and my television programme interesting.
Level 3	Level 4	Level 5

3

Britain: Union and conflict

Objectives

At the end of this unit you will be able to:

- describe the ways conflict led to the creation of modern Britain and Ireland

Today the British Isles contain two countries: the United Kingdom and the Republic of Ireland. Both countries are members of the European Union. The period 1500 to the early 20th century was a period of great change, during which the British Isles were united into one country, and then divided into two.

The Battle of Culloden, 16 April 1746

This is an image of the Battle of Culloden of 1746, the last battle ever to be fought on British soil. It was an important event in the attempt to create a single country that would unite the British Isles.

The picture helps show how the history of Britain from 1500 to the early 20th century involved conflict. Although Culloden was the last battle in Britain, it wasn't the last example of conflict, which recurred throughout the history of Britain and Ireland, from 1500 to the 20th century.

For example, from 1603, England and Scotland were united under one king. But not everyone in Scotland was happy with the union between the two countries. This unit explores how conflict shaped the creation of modern Britain.

Questions

1 Describe what is happening in the picture.
2 What message do you think the picture is trying to give?
3 Why do you think the history of the British Isles from 1500 to the early 20th century involved conflict?

The growth of Britain 1500–1918

In the period 1500-1918, there were significant developments in Britain. We are going to examine the importance of these changes, and how they contributed to the growth of Britain.

The Act of Union, 1707

Getting you thinking

Britain changed in many ways between 1500 and 1918. There were dramatic changes in technology, for example. Can you think of any other ways Britain changed?

Reformation: A period of religious reform in the 16th century
Protestantism: a form of Christianity that rejected the Catholic Church

After Henry VIII (1509–1547) began the *Reformation* of the English church, more people rejected the Catholic Church and supported *Protestantism*. Then the Catholic Stuarts came to power in England in 1603. King Charles I (1625–1649) clashed with parliament over religion and power. This led to the English Civil War of 1642-1648, which parliament won. Charles I was beheaded in 1649 and parliament ruled England from 1649 to 1653. Oliver Cromwell then ruled from 1653 to 1658, as Lord Protector. In 1660, parliament decided to restore the monarchy, and invited Charles II to become the king.

The Stuart line of kings ended in 1688 with the Glorious Revolution. James II was a Catholic, who was feared by powerful Protestants. So in 1688 they invited William of Orange and his wife Mary, the Princess Royal, to become the King and Queen of England. James II fled to France. In 1707 Scotland was united with England and Wales through the Act of Union, which ended Scottish independence.

In the 18th and 19th century, parliament's power increased. The majority of people, however, could not vote for their government. So, in the 19th century, campaigners such as the *Chartists* demanded more political reforms. The Great Reform Act of 1832 and the 1884 Reform Act extended the vote to more adult men. Women, however, were not allowed to vote until the Representation of the Peoples Act in 1918.

From 1500 to 1918, there were dramatic technological changes. In the 16th century roads and transport were very poor. It took six and a half days to travel between London and Newcastle by stage coach in 1750. Roads improved in the 18th century, with the introduction of turnpikes and toll houses, where people were charged for using the roads.

The growth of industry in the 18th and 19th centuries depended on the transport of goods around the country. More canals were built in the 18th century, such as the Bridgewater Canal between Liverpool and Manchester. In the 19th century, steam trains and steam ships further improved transport. The building of railway lines, such as the Liverpool and Manchester Railway, reduced transport costs. Goods became cheaper, and demand for them increased. This encouraged trade and sparked the changes which became known as the *Industrial Revolution* (1730–1850). Motorised vehicles and aeroplanes appeared in the early 20th century. Although these technologies could be used for peaceful means, they were also used for warfare during World War One (1914–1918) and World War Two (1939–1945).

Now it's your turn

1 Note down important dates in the text and create a timeline in the correct chronological order.
2 From the text select one example of an important political, religious and technological change. Explain why you think each of these changes was important.

Check your progress

☆ I can describe different events that contributed to the growth of Britain from 1500 to 1918.
☆☆ I can explain the importance of these events.
☆☆☆ I can explain links between different events.

Chartists: campaigners for political and social change in the mid-19th century
Industrial Revolution: the rapid change to Britain's economy in the 18th and 19th centuries

England and Wales in Tudor times

Objectives

By the end of the lesson you will be able to:

- explain the powers Henry VIII used to rule
- decide whether Henry VIII used his power successfully

The Tudors ruled from 1485 to 1603. Henry VIII (1509–1547) had both successes and failures as a ruler.

Getting you thinking

- What qualities do you think would make a successful ruler during the Tudor period?

King Henry the eyght.

Henry VIII needed money and good advisers to rule successfully. The Council was the centre of royal power. Its most important advisers were called the Privy Council. The gentry acted as *justices of the peace*, helping Henry rule the countryside. In *court*, nobles competed to gain influence with the king to increase their own power.

Henry disliked the everyday business of government. He relied heavily on advisers such as Sir Thomas Wolsey. Henry wanted Wolsey to make England an important power. Wolsey believed England should be the peacemaker between European monarchs and organised spectacular meetings. In 1520 Henry met King Francis I in France. A temporary town of extravagant tents and a palace of painted canvas and wood decorated in jewels were erected. This famous event was called the Field of the Cloth of Gold.

King Henry VIII in parliament

Justices of the peace: officers who enforced the king's law
Court: the powerful people who surrounded the king

In 1527 Henry wanted to divorce Catherine of Aragon because she had not provided him with a male *heir*. Wolsey asked the Pope to grant Henry a divorce but the Pope refused, fearful of the powerful king of Spain, who was related to Catherine. Wolsey was arrested and dismissed as chancellor. Sir Thomas More became the new chancellor. In 1529 Henry called a meeting of parliament. Aware that many people disliked the corruption of the Catholic Church and resented paying *tithes*, Henry, supported by Thomas Cromwell, began an attack on the power of the Catholic Church.

First Henry appointed Thomas Cranmer as the new Archbishop of Canterbury. Cranmer granted Henry a divorce from Catherine allowing Henry to marry Anne Boleyn in 1533. Then, in 1534, the Act of Supremacy made Henry the Head of the Church in England, instead of the Pope. All money paid to the new Church of England now went to the royal treasury. Sir Thomas More, who had opposed this decision, was executed.

During 1536–1539 Henry dissolved the *monasteries*. The wealth of the monasteries went to the king's treasury. In 1536 Robert Aske led a rebellion against the closures of the monasteries. Aske entered negotiations with the Duke of Norfolk and Henry promised to listen to his demands. The rebels disbanded, but in 1537 Norfolk arrested the leaders of the rebellion and executed over 200 rebels.

In 1536 Wales was divided into counties with justices of the peace to ensure that the king's power was not threatened. The closure of the monasteries increased Henry's wealth and power. Cromwell ensured that the Privy Council became the most powerful group in England and Wales. In the 1540s Henry was threatened by Catholic countries. Cromwell wanted alliances with Protestant countries and arranged Henry's marriage with Anne of Cleves. The marriage was a disaster and Cromwell was executed.

Check your progress

I can talk about how Henry VIII ruled.
I can explain his strengths and weaknesses.
I can decide whether or not his rule was successful, and give reasons.

Now it's your turn

Create a timeline of events during the reign of Henry VIII.

Heir: the next in line to the throne   *Tithes:* a tax paid to the church
Monasteries: places where monks live and follow a religious life

Union of England and Scotland 1603–1707

Until 1707 Scotland remained an independent country. There were many reasons for Scotland joining the United Kingdom.

Getting you thinking

- What benefits came from closer unity between England and Scotland?

Unification in 1707 was caused by religion, and a desire for peace and trade. In 1603 James I became King of England and Scotland. Scotland, however, remained independent. Scotland had its own parliament, privy council and *kirk*. James I did not allow the Scots full trading rights with England. Scottish merchants paid taxes on goods they brought into England. The Scots were denied trading rights with the growing British Empire.

In 1637 the Scots rebelled against Charles I and invaded England. He had tried to force a new prayer book on the Scottish *Presbyterian* kirk. Charles signed a treaty with the Scots because the English parliament refused to support him. A civil war (1642–1649) began between Charles I and parliament. The Scots initially supported the English parliament. In 1646 Charles surrendered to the Scots, who handed him over to the English parliament. In 1648 Charles I agreed a secret deal with the Scots. The Scots would invade England to restore Charles I to power in return for an English Presbyterian church. The *Royalist* and Scottish forces were defeated at the Battle of Preston in 1648.

Parliament executed Charles I in 1649. The Scots decided to crown his son, Prince Charles, the king of Scotland. Oliver Cromwell saw this as a threat and invaded Scotland. He defeated Scottish forces at the Battle of Dunbar in 1650. In 1651 the Scots invaded England and were defeated at the Battle of Worcester. Charles fled Scotland and English soldiers then occupied Scotland. The Scottish parliament was closed but trade improved. Scottish merchants could trade more freely with England and her colonies.

Kirk: the Scottish church
Presbyterian: follower of a branch of Protestantism

In 1660 Charles II became King of England and Scotland, ruling until 1685. James II (1685–1688) allowed the Scots to keep their own parliament and kirk. However he was removed in the Glorious Revolution of 1688, and the English parliament invited William III (1689–1702) to become the new king. William forced all Scots to swear an oath of loyalty to him by 1692. Queen Anne (1702–1714) had no heir. The English parliament turned to the House of Hanover in Germany to provide an heir. Some Scots realised that closer union with England would bring more trade and wealth. The English realised that closer union would prevent Scotland making alliances with enemies such as France.

A portrait of King James I

In 1707 the Act of Union was passed. Forty-five Scottish MPs and 16 Scottish lords entered parliament in London. It was agreed that George of Hanover would become king. The Scots kept control of their own Presbyterian kirk. There were opponents to the Union in both England and Wales.

Now it's your turn APP

You are an English Protestant merchant in 1707. Write a letter to a Scottish Protestant merchant, giving reasons why Scots should support an Act of Union between England and Scotland.

Check your progress

I can describe different events leading to the Act of Union.
I can explain why it happened.
I can decide what was the most important cause, and give reasons.

Royalists: supporters of Charles I during the Civil War

Glencoe 1692: case study

In 1692 King William III attempted to increase his power within Scotland. We are going to explore the impact of his actions and the reaction of some Scots to his policies.

Getting you thinking

- Why do you think some Scots opposed closer union with England?

After the Glorious Revolution of 1688 William III knew some *Highland* Scottish clans still supported the old king, James II. In 1691 William III ordered all Scottish clans to swear an oath of loyalty to him by New Year's Day the following year. Maclain Macdonald, the chief of the MacDonald *clan*, travelled from Glencoe to Fort William to take his oath. When he reached Fort William the Governor told him he had to make his oath in front of the sheriff at Inverary about 60 miles away.

A painting of the Massacre at Glencoe

Highland: coming from a region in the northwest of Scotland

Clan: A group of families with a common surname

When MacDonald reached Inverary, the sheriff was away celebrating *Hogmanay*. Therefore MacDonald could not take his oath until 6 January 1692. William III decided that the MacDonald clan had to be punished to set an example to the other Highland clans. He ordered 120 soldiers to be placed in the homes of the MacDonald clan in Glencoe. Most of the troops were from the Campbell clan, the sworn enemies of the MacDonalds.

Highland custom stated that feuding between clans had to be stopped when one clan was showing hospitality to another. The Campbells lived with the MacDonalds for two weeks. After two weeks the soldiers were ordered to kill all MacDonald men, women and children under the age of 70. The *massacre* started at 5am on 13 February 1692. Afterwards 38 bodies were found. The majority of the MacDonalds escaped but some froze to death.

The massacre caused more Highlanders to support James II and his descendants as the rightful kings of Scotland. The MacDonald chief felt betrayed by the English and the Campbell clan. William III's Scottish troops had carried out the massacre and many highlanders held him directly responsible for it.

A group of men were appointed to investigate the massacre. William III was found innocent of any involvement even though he had countersigned the orders. The Scottish parliament, however, after reading the report of the investigation, declared that the MacDonald men had been murdered. They also recommended punishments for the men who had planned the killings. These recommendations, however, were largely ignored and only John Campbell, the Earl of Breadalbane, spent a few days imprisoned in Edinburgh Castle. The fact that no-one was severely punished for the massacre increased the hatred some Highland Scots felt for the English and for King William.

Now it's your turn

Imagine you are a member of the MacDonald clan. Design a wanted poster for those responsible for the massacre.

Check your progress

I can describe the events leading up to the Glencoe massacre.
I can describe the events of the massacre.
I can explain some of the consequences of the Glencoe massacre.

Hogmanay: Scottish New Year
Massacre: The killing of a large group of people

The Jacobite rebellions

Objectives

By the end of this lesson you will be able to:

- explain the causes of the Jacobite rebellions of 1715 and 1745
- explain the different consequences of the rebellions

During the early 18th century many Scots opposed the Act of Union. Many wanted the Stuarts to become the kings of Scotland. This resulted in rebellions, which had numerous consequences.

Getting you thinking

- Why did the Jacobite rebels fail to end the Union?

In 1715 James Edward Stuart, the son of James II, claimed the throne of Scotland. Lowland Scots generally supported the Act of Union. Some viewed Highland Scots with hostility. Highland Scots were Catholic, whilst Lowland Scots were Presbyterians. Many Highland Scots did not like being ruled from London and supported the return of James. Some Highlanders planned a rebellion, and were known as *Jacobites*.

Queen Anne died in 1715 and left no heirs to the throne. The Jacobites saw this as an opportunity for the Stuarts to return. The English parliament invited Prince George of the House of Hanover to become king. He was not popular and could only speak German. A Scottish lord, the Earl of Mar, led a rebellion against George I. He wanted Scottish independence. On 6 September 1715 he started the rebellion, demanding the return of James Edward Stuart to the throne.

The beheading of the rebel lords, 1746

Jacobite: A Scottish rebel, named after the Latin word 'Jacobus' meaning James

On 13 November 1715 the rebels fought against the Duke of Argyll near Stirling. Neither side won the battle. In December James arrived in Scotland. The Earl of Mar convinced James to leave Scotland. He feared James would be captured. This signalled the end of the rebellion. King George remained the king of England and Scotland.

In 1745 there was a second rebellion. Many Scots disliked having to pay taxes to the government in London. Highlanders wanted the Stuarts to return to the throne. France was at war with England. In 1744 King Louis XV supported the Stuart claim to the throne. The Stuarts were based in Paris. Bonnie Prince Charlie, known as the *Young Pretender*, landed in Scotland in July 1745 to join the rebellion. The rebellion in 1745 failed, but it had come closer to success than the rebellion of 1715.

The 1745 rebellion had several consequences. After victory the English army, led by the Duke of Cumberland, marched through the Highlands of Scotland, killing large numbers of Highlanders. They hoped to capture Bonnie Prince Charlie but he escaped to France in 1746.

King George II (1727–1760) and his parliament were determined to prevent another rebellion in Scotland. They attempted to destroy the clan system. All clan members had to surrender their weapons. They could no longer wear clan tartan. The Hanoverian rule over Scotland and England was never threatened again. By the end of the 18th century successful industries had emerged in the Lowlands. Glasgow and Edinburgh became wealthy trading centres.

Now it's your turn

Write a short account of the causes of these rebellions, and on their consequences for Scotland.

Check your progress

I can explain the causes and consequences of the rebellions.
I can explain their importance.
I can explain how the causes linked together to cause the rebellions.

Young Pretender: James Edward Stuart was called the 'Old Pretender'. His son was called the 'Young Pretender' or 'Bonnie Prince Charlie'

Bonnie Prince Charlie and Culloden

Objectives

By the end of this lesson you will be able to:

- explain the role of Bonnie Prince Charlie in the 1745 rebellion
- decide if he was a hero or poor leader

Bonnie Prince Charlie wanted his father, James Edward Stuart, to be king of Scotland and England. Some have viewed him as a hero. Others have blamed him for bringing death and destruction to the Highlands.

- Why did some Scots support Bonnie Prince Charlie?

In July 1745 Bonnie Prince Charlie landed in Scotland. He made his way to Glenfinnan where he called for Scots to support his rebellion. He gained support from some Scottish clans. Soon he had an army of about 4,000 men.

He marched on Edinburgh where many people supported the Stuarts. In September 1745 his army clashed with the English army led by General Cope. The *Highlanders* won the battle and they now controlled most of Scotland.

Many of his supporters advised him to stay in Scotland. He decided to march into England, however, because he believed English Catholics would support him. His forces reached Derby but only 300 Englishmen joined him. None were from powerful Catholic families. At Derby his advisers wanted him to retreat to Scotland. Many of his Highland troops wanted to return to their farms. Meanwhile George II and his supporters in London were panicking and planning to leave London, but the Scottish rebels never knew this.

Charles Edward Stuart – 'Bonnie Prince Charlie'

Highlanders: Scots who live in north-west Scotland

Bonnie Prince Charlie wanted to march to London. His advisers, however, convinced him to retreat. His soldiers were cold, hungry and being pursued by an English army. His forces reached Scotland in December 1745.

In Scotland the rebels divided their forces to make it more difficult for the English troops. Small groups of Highlanders began deserting his army. The son of George II, the Duke of Cumberland, pursued the rebels. His army was well equipped and trained. His mission was to crush the rebellion.

The Highlanders again supported Bonnie Prince Charlie. The two armies met at Culloden Moor near Inverness. He was advised by Lord George Murray to place his troops on soft ground, which would make it much more difficult for British cavalry charges. He ignored this advice and ordered his troops to remain on firmer ground. Cumberland's army was well supplied, whilst the rebels had food shortages and difficulties with supplies. They were also outnumbered. The rebels lost the battle and 1,200 Jacobites were killed, whilst the Duke of Cumberland only lost 76 men.

Bonnie Prince Charlie escaped the battle. He was pursued by English forces for five months. A woman called Flora MacDonald helped him to escape by dressing him as a female servant. He was rowed 20 miles to the Isle of Skye, from where he escaped to France. The English smashed the power of the Highland clan chiefs and the Stuarts never threatened the union between England and Scotland again.

Now it's your turn

Design a poster which supports the Stuart claim to the throne of Scotland.

Check your progress

I can explain how the 1745 rebellion started.
I can explain who led and supported the rebellion.
I can explain the role of Bonnie Prince Charlie in the rebellion's failure.

Britain & Ireland 1500–1800

Relations between Britain and Ireland changed between 1500 and 1800, often because of different religious beliefs and arguments over who should control Ireland. These changes caused rebellions and wars.

Getting you thinking

In the period 1500–1800 there were many violent clashes between the Irish and English.

- What do you think the causes of these clashes might have been?

In the 1530s Henry VIII supported religious reforms against the Catholic Church. The Irish Catholics disliked his reforms. They attempted a rebellion in 1534. By 1541, however, the Irish were forced to accept Henry VIII (1509–1547) as king. Although Edward VI (1547–1553) had strengthened Protestantism in England, Catholicism remained strong in Ireland. Elizabeth I (1558–1603) increased her control over Ireland by sending English settlers to Ireland. In 1607, after a failed Irish rebellion, James I (1603–1625) sent more settlers and they established the *Plantation of Ulster*. In 1603 Catholics owned 90 per cent of the land, but by 1750 this had fallen to five per cent.

In 1641 the Irish rebelled against Charles I (1625–1649). Approximately 3,000 Protestant settlers were killed. The English Civil War (1642–1649) distracted England from Ireland. However, after the execution of Charles I in 1649, Oliver Cromwell led an army to crush the Irish. He was very brutal and brought more land under Protestant control. In September 1649 Cromwell attacked the Irish town of Drogheda, to crush a rebellion against English rule that had broken out. Over 2,000 people were killed in Drogheda by English troops.

After losing his throne in 1688 James II (1685–1688) turned to King Louis XIV. He provided a French army, which James II took to Ireland. James II gave land back to Irish Catholics. However, King William III (1688-1702) of England sent an army to crush James II. They met at the River Boyne on 1 July 1690. The forces of James II were defeated. English troops established control over Ireland. The English parliament passed *penal laws* against the Catholics in Ireland; for example, no Catholics could be lawyers.

Objectives

By the end of the lesson you will be able to:

- describe events which shaped relations between Britain and Ireland
- explain the significance of different events and individuals

1641

1703

- 0–24% Catholic owned
- 25–49% Catholic owned
- 50–100% Catholic owned

By the end of the seventeenth century, only five per cent of Irish land was owned by Catholics
Credit: www.irelandstory.com

Plantation of Ulster: Land given to English and Scottish settlers in Ireland
Penal Laws: Harsh laws which the English used to control the Irish

During the 18th century Ireland remained largely peaceful. Towards the end of the 18th century, however, more Irishmen wanted increased political power. In the 18th century the Irish had their own parliament in Dublin. The Irish parliament had limited power over the Irish government, which mostly consisted of Englishmen appointed by the parliament in London. In the 1770s George III relaxed some penal laws. The English were fighting American rebels and feared a rebellion in Ireland. In 1789 the French Revolution took place, which resulted in the spreading of radical ideas. These events caused more Irishmen – both Catholic and Protestant – to demand more political power in the 1790s.

William of Orange at the Battle of the Boyne

Now it's your turn

Explain how different individuals had an impact on relations between Britain and Ireland.

Check your progress

⭐ I can talk about some important events in the period 1500–1800.
⭐⭐ I understand the role of different individuals.
⭐⭐⭐ I can explain the importance of individuals and events in changing relations between Britain and Ireland.

The 1798 Rebellion and the Union of Britain and Ireland

Objectives

By the end of this lesson you will be able to:

- describe the causes of the 1798 Rebellion
- explain what led to the Union of Britain and Ireland

In 1791 a group called the United Irishmen emerged, led by Theobald Wolfe Tone. They opposed the way Ireland was being governed.

Getting you thinking

- When do you think violence can be justified in removing a government?

The United Irishmen consisted of different groups and all disliked the way Ireland was ruled. *Presbyterian* Protestants located mostly in *Ulster* disliked the penal laws. They invited Tone to Ulster and in 1791 the United Irishmen were established. Many Protestants like Tone found their career paths limited because they lacked powerful English connections. Catholics also disliked the penal laws; for example, they could not own a horse valued above £5.

Tone believed the penal laws kept the Irish divided. In August 1791 he published a pamphlet. He argued Catholics should be treated the same as Protestants. Tone became famous and popular with Irish Catholics and Protestants. Support for the United Irishmen spread across Ireland. They demanded the ending of the penal laws and reform of the Irish parliament in Dublin. They also wanted the Dublin parliament to be able to pass laws free from English interference.

The United Irishmen saw themselves as defending liberty and ending corrupt government. Many of them were inspired by the success and ideas of the American Revolution (1776–1783) and the French Revolution of 1789. Initially the United Irishmen had some successes, such as in 1792, when Catholics were allowed to become lawyers.

However, from 1792 onwards Britain was at war with the new *revolutionary* government in France. The English government was frightened by new radical ideas such as liberty for all. Men like Tone were viewed as being dangerous traitors. The government tightened their control over Ulster. Tone had connections with the new French government and had to leave Ireland. He stopped being a reformer and became a revolutionary.

Presbyterian: Protestant church in Ireland
Ulster: A province in the north of Ireland

He first went to America and then France where he gained support for an Irish rebellion. In 1796 he joined a French invasion fleet of Ireland, which failed due to bad weather. In 1798 the British increased their clampdown on the whole of Ireland. This resulted in rebellion across Ireland. Some of the most serious fighting took place in Ulster. Tone appealed for French support but not enough was provided and the rebellion failed. Tone was captured by the British in 1798 and he killed himself in jail.

The United Irishmen in training

The British prime minister, William Pitt the Younger, decided that Ireland needed to be ruled directly from London. Pitt supported an Act of Union with Ireland. He was prepared to allow Catholics to sit in parliament in England if they accepted the Act of Union. In January 1801 the Act of Union was passed. The act allowed 100 MPs and 32 lords to sit in the Westminster parliament.

Now it's your turn

Imagine you are an Irish rebel. Write a speech criticising the British government.

Check your progress

I know who supported the rebellion.
I can explain why the rebellion started.
I can explain how the rebellion led to the Act of Union.

Revolutionary: Someone who wants complete political change, and is prepared to use violence

The Irish Famine 1845–1849

Objectives

By the end of this lesson you will be able to

- describe and explain the different causes of the Irish Famine
- identify different consequences of the famine

Between 1845 and 1849 Ireland suffered a *famine*. Potatoes were the main source of food but were destroyed by a disease called 'blight'. The consequences of the famine were severe in Ireland, especially in rural areas.

Getting you thinking

- Famines still happen today. Some famines are man-made and some are caused by nature. How do you think famines could be prevented?

Many charities helped people during the famine. Both the Catholic and Protestant churches tried to help the victims. Blight destroyed potato crops in 1846, 1847 and 1848. More help was needed. The Irish population had risen in the early 19th century. In 1841 it was 8.2 million.

Initially the British government did not supply enough help, which made the famine worse. The government did not understand the severity of the famine; in Britain the government only helped people in return for work. In Ireland most people were too weak to work. Over a million Irish died from starvation and diseases.

Victims of the famine are carted away at Skibbereen in southern Ireland, 1847

Famine: When food becomes extremely scarce and people die from starvation and disease

Distribution of clothing to a poor family, during the 1847 famine

Many Irish peasant farmers could not afford to buy food. During the famine Ireland continued to export meat and dairy produce. The British press revealed the horrors of the famine. Prime Minister Peel helped the Irish by passing a law in May 1846 to end the *Corn Laws*. It was hoped that free trade would allow cheaper food into Ireland. Peel also imported £100,000 of American corn into Ireland.

In 1846, however, Peel's government collapsed over the ending of the Corn Laws. Peel was replaced by Lord John Russell. Russell did not share Peel's view that the government should help the Irish. Life became very hard in Ireland. When people became too ill to work and could not pay their rent, they were often evicted by their landlords. Many people became homeless. Some people even resorted to eating dead bodies. Some Irish landlords tried to help their tenants but many provided no help.

During the famine over a million Irish *emigrated*. In 1851 a census revealed that there were two million fewer people living in Ireland as compared to 1845. Many emigrated to countries such as Australia and Canada. The majority settled in the USA. Conditions on the ships to the USA were very cramped and harsh. Diseases were common on these ships and they became known as coffin ships. After the famine many Irish people believed the union between Britain and Ireland was a failure. Many Irishmen in the USA became powerful and wealthy opponents of the union.

Now it's your turn

The Irish famine had both short- and long-term consequences. After reading the text:
1 Can you identify short-term consequences of the famine?
2 Can you identify long-term consequences of the famine?
3 What do you think are the most important consequences of the famine?

Check your progress

★ I can explain how the famine started.
★★ I can explain why the famine was so severe.
★★★ I can explain the causes and consequences of the famine.

Corn Laws: A tax on foreign wheat imported into Britain
Emigration: People leaving one country to settle in another country

Irish emigration

During the 19th century large numbers of Irish people *emigrated*. Some settled in Britain, many moved to the USA, Australia or Canada. There were many reasons why they left Ireland.

Getting you thinking

- Why do you think the USA would have been a popular choice for Irish emigrants in the 19th and early 20th century?

Between 1815 and 1845 about 1.5 million Irish people emigrated. The majority of people in this period remained in Ireland, due to close ties to the land they helped farm, or to their families. The famine of 1845–1849 caused a further 1.5 million people to emigrate during these years. Between 1850 and 1910 another 4.5 million people emigrated. A key reason why Irish people emigrated was to seek a better life abroad. Many disliked the union with Britain. However, many went to England and Scotland where the Industrial Revolution had created demand for workers.

Many emigrated to seek jobs and land in the USA. In the USA there was more opportunity to own land. Before 1845 the majority of people who emigrated were often single and landless men, who could just afford a single place on a ship to the USA or Canada. The famine of 1845–1849 was a turning point, after which many more Irish people, including whole families, emigrated.

The British government failed to provide enough help for Irish peasants during the Irish famine. In addition, *evictions* from the land caused many to seek improved lives in the USA. In 1851 alone, 250,000 emigrants left Ireland for the Americas. Even wealthier Irish farmers began to emigrate due to increased taxes and declining profits. However, the majority of people who left Ireland after 1850 were the rural poor from southern Ireland. Another important difference was that whole families were now emigrating instead of individuals. Larger farms were established in Ireland after 1850 to increase profits. Therefore less land was available for people to farm and live on.

Emigrate: To leave one country and settle in another country
Eviction: The forceful removal of a person from their home or land

Irish emigrants on board ship, 1850

Many emigrants found it difficult to raise the money for tickets on the ships. Some were given money by their old *landlords* who wanted them off their land, and some borrowed money from friends or family already in America. The ships that transported them were known as 'coffin ships' and the emigrants travelled in horrific conditions. The journey lasted for approximately 40 days and about 20 per cent of emigrants died before reaching America.

Now it's your turn

Design a 19th-century poster promoting different reasons why people should emigrate from Ireland to the USA . Use the above text and the internet for ideas to put in your poster.

Check your progress

★ I know when and where people emigrated to from Ireland.

★★ I can explain why the Irish emigrated and the importance of the famine of 1845–1849.

★★★ I can explore links between various causes and explain how the Irish famine was a turning point.

Landlord: A person who lets land or property for profit

The Fenians

In 1858 the Irish *Republican* Brotherhood was established in both Ireland and the USA. This group was also known as the Fenians. They believed violence was the most effective way to persuade Britain to end the Union and grant independence to Ireland.

Getting you thinking

- Why do you think men such as James Stephens resorted to violence to achieve their political goals?

A poster commemorating three Fenians who were executed in England

Republican: Irish supporters of independence.
Mortal sin: one which means the sinner will go to hell when they die

The Fenians were a secret organisation. They organised themselves into small groups which they hoped would prevent them being discovered by British spies. However, some groups of Fenians were very large and were easily *infiltrated*. Therefore British and Irish supporters of the Union had detailed knowledge about Fenian activities and membership. Not all Irish Catholics supported the Fenians and their use of violence. The Archbishop of Dublin, Father Paul Cullen, declared membership of the Fenians a '*mortal sin*'.

James Stephens, the leader of the Fenians in Ireland, ran a popular newspaper called *The Irish People* which was banned by the British in 1865. He struggled to organise a widespread Irish rebellion. He was weakened by divisions amongst Fenians in America over tactics to end the Union. These delays caused people to leave the Fenians. Stephens was eventually removed as leader. The rebellion finally took place in 1867 but failed and was quickly crushed. Rebellions in Dublin and Cork were poorly led and organised.

The Fenians then launched *terrorist* attacks on mainland Britain in 1867, which attracted publicity for their cause. In Manchester three Irishmen were hanged after helping two Fenian prisoners escape. They became known as the Manchester Martyrs. In December there was an attempt to rescue a Fenian who was in Clerkenwell Prison in London. The Fenian volunteers tried to blow a hole in the prison wall. Twelve people were killed and fifty injured.

After these events the Fenian movement declined. However, they had some impact on the British government. Prime Minister William Gladstone passed reforms to ease tensions in Ireland. These reforms also gained the support of English Catholic voters. He passed the 1870 Land Act, which was designed to protect tenants who were wrongly evicted. Gladstone believed the Irish had genuine grievances, which had to be solved if Ireland was to be an effective member of the Union. However Gladstone's reforms were not designed to end the Act of Union, which many Irish disliked.

Now it's your turn

Imagine you are Irish and are opposed to the use of violence. What advice would you give to the Fenians to convince them to reject violence as a method to achieve their political goals?

Check your progress

⭐ I can explain who the Fenians were.

⭐⭐ I can explain what their aims and methods were.

⭐⭐⭐ I can explain both the successes and failures of the Fenians.

Infiltrate: To join a group or organisation in order to find out information and destroy it
Terrorist: A person who uses violence to achieve their political aims

Parnell and Home Rule

Objectives

By the end of the lesson you will be able to

- explain the meaning of Home Rule

- describe the role of Parnell in strengthening demands for Home Rule in Ireland

In the 1880s Charles Stewart Parnell, a Protestant Irish MP, became the leader of the *Home Rule Party*, also known as the 'New Departure'. He united different groups in Ireland.

Charles Stewart Parnell

Getting you thinking

- Imagine you are Parnell, pictured above. How would you persuade the Irish population to support your peaceful methods of achieving Home Rule? How would you persuade them to reject the use of violence?

Home Rule: *Ireland would rule itself from its own parliament but remain part of the British Empire*

During the 1870s, Irish farmers suffered difficult economic conditions. Prices were falling and many farmers were evicted. Parnell became the president of the Land League. The league campaigned for laws to protect tenants against landlords and for financial support for poor farmers to buy land. Parnell realised this organisation could increase support for Home Rule. Parnell supported peaceful protests and did not support the use of violence. In 1882 the British government agreed the Kilmainham Treaty with Parnell. This resulted in the release of people involved in Land League protests and more government aid to poor farmers.

A week after the signing of the treaty, two leading British politicians were assassinated in Dublin, by a terrorist group known as the 'Invincibles'. Parnell used this event as a reason to leave the Land League, which had become more influenced by Fenians and supporters of violent methods. Parnell then established the Irish National League, which focused on achieving Home Rule through peaceful political methods.

After the 1885 elections Parnell became the head of 86 MPs in the Westminster parliament. He convinced Gladstone, the prime minister, to support the passing of a Home Rule Bill through parliament, but the bill was not passed. Many MPs opposed Home Rule. Some feared it would signal the break-up of the British Empire. Opposition also emerged from Protestants who lived in *Ulster*. They feared that Catholics would dominate an Irish government. In 1886 they set up the Unionist Party to prevent Home Rule.

In 1889 Parnell's influence declined. He was named in a divorce case because he had an affair with a colleague's wife. The scandal split his party and Parnell died in 1891. In 1893 the Liberal Party attempted to pass another Home Rule Bill, which failed. Parnell had succeeded in increasing support for Home Rule. However, the tensions between Ireland and Britain had still not been resolved.

Now it's your turn APP

Imagine you are Parnell. Write two speeches.
1 One speech should be aimed at convincing the Irish to support you and your goal of Home Rule.
2 The second speech should be aimed at the British government and Gladstone to convince them to support the passing of Home Rule through the British parliament.

Check your progress

★ I can explain the meaning of Home Rule.

★★ I can explain the role of Parnell in seeking Home Rule.

★★★ I can explain the importance of Parnell.

Ulster: One of the four provinces of Ireland

The Easter Rising

Objectives

By the end of this lesson you will be able to:

- describe the events of the 1916 Easter Rising
- explain both the successes and failures of the 1916 Easter Rising

On 24 April 1916 the Irish Volunteers, led by James Connolly, and the Irish Citizen Army, led by Patrick Pearse, attempted to seize control of Dublin. Both groups wanted independence for Ireland. People have viewed the 1916 Easter Rising both as a success and as a failure.

Getting you thinking

- Look at the image below, which is a modern march celebrating and remembering the rebels of 1916. Many within Ireland see the rebels involved in the 1916 Easter Rising as heroes. Why do you think this is the case?

Just before the Easter Rising the *rebels* were hoping to receive a shipment of weapons from Germany. This had been organised by Sir Roger Casement. The weapons were purchased with money provided by Irish Americans. The British Navy prevented the weapons from reaching the rebels. The British authorities arrested Casement.

A march commemorating the Easter Rising in Dublin

Rebel: In this case someone who uses violence to end the Union of Ireland and Great Britain

The rebels decided to continue with the rebellion. Pearse knew the rebellion would probably fail. However, he believed the deaths of rebels would create *martyrs* and inspire the Irish population to support the struggle for Irish independence. He called this idea the 'blood sacrifice'.

On Easter Monday 1916, around 2,000 rebels seized control of the General Post Office building (GPO). Pearse read out the Irish Proclamation of Independence on the stairs of the building. The British used artillery and a gunboat, which was on the River Liffey, to attack the rebels in the GPO. Within one week the rebels surrendered.

During the fighting 64 rebels, 220 civilians and 130 British soldiers and police were killed. Initially the majority of the Irish population were appalled by the rebellion. The Catholic Church condemned the rebellion. The rebels were marched through Dublin by the British Army and the local population jeered the rebels.

The British were at war with Germany in 1916 and felt betrayed by the rebellion. The British authorities executed leaders of the rebellion. This created sympathy for the rebels in Ireland. The British government also introduced *martial law* and imprisoned suspected rebel sympathisers. Many innocent people were arrested by the British. These actions increased support for the Sinn Fein political party. They became determined to achieve an independent Ireland. Support for accepting only Home Rule declined in Ireland. The rebellion also frightened Protestants in Ulster. They became more determined to keep Ulster as a part of the United Kingdom.

Now it's your turn

Imagine you are a journalist writing in the late 1920s. Write a magazine article explaining the successes and failures of the 1916 Easter Rising. You should use the above text for ideas.

You may wish to carry out extra research on the internet.

Check your progress

I can explain when the 1916 Easter Rising started.
I can explain the role and actions of the Irish rebels.
I can explain the successes and failures of the Easter Rising.

Martyrs: A person who is killed for their beliefs
Martial law: When military law is introduced

The division of Ireland, 1920–1922

In 1922 The British government *partitioned* Ireland. The majority of Irish Protestants supported the Union. However, many Irish *nationalists*, who were mostly Catholics, supported independence.

'The kindest cut of all', a 1920 cartoon showing Lloyd George carrying out the Partition of Ireland

Getting you thinking

- Why do you think the majority of the Irish population and the British government supported partition in 1922? How was Northern Ireland different from the rest of Ireland?

In 1918 Sinn Fein had the most Irish MPs in the Westminster parliament. In 1919 Sinn Fein MPs declared themselves the government of Ireland. They ignored British rule and established the Irish Republican Army (IRA). Ulster, populated mostly by Protestants, remained loyal to Britain.

Nationalist: a supporter of a country's independence
Partition: Division into different parts

The Sinn Fein leader Eamon de Valera supported violence against British forces. Led by Michael Collins, the IRA began a *guerrilla war* against the police, the Royal Irish Constabulary. Britain sent troops to Ireland to support the Irish police. Some of these troops were called 'Black and Tans'. All sides committed brutal killings. The Black and Tans killed and tortured IRA suspects. The IRA killed Protestant farmers. This resulted in attacks on Catholic families in Belfast.

In 1920 Lloyd George, the British prime minister, introduced the Government of Ireland Act. The act allowed six of Ulster's nine counties to become self-governing with a parliament in Belfast. The remaining 26 counties would have their parliament in Dublin. Britain would control the Irish military and naval bases. The IRA rejected the act and the guerrilla war continued.

Lloyd George was determined to end the conflict. Britain was still recovering from the cost of World War One. Fighting the IRA was very expensive. The American government criticised Britain for not allowing Irish independence. In 1921 a truce was agreed between Britain and the IRA.

The Anglo-Irish treaty was signed, which had many consequences. The 26 counties of Ireland became the Irish Free State. All British forces were withdrawn. The Irish Free State created its own army, currency and flag. The six counties of Northern Ireland were not included in the Irish Free State. The Irish Free State remained a part of the British Empire.

The majority of people voted for the treaty in 1922 because they wanted peace. However, De Valera and some members of the IRA rejected the treaty. A brutal civil war broke out in the Irish Free State, which lasted until 1923. Throughout the 20th century tensions remained high between Catholics and Protestants in Northern Ireland.

Now it's your turn

Design two posters. One poster should support the partition of Ireland. When designing the poster imagine you are an Irish Protestant living in Belfast who supports partition. The second poster should be opposed to partition. For this poster, imagine you are an Irish Catholic who wants Ireland to remain a united country.

Check your progress

I can explain when and how Ireland was partitioned.
I can explain the causes and consequences of partition.
I can explain the most important cause and consequence of partition.

Guerrilla warfare: Small groups of fighters who launch surprise attacks

What was the most significant event in the growth of Britain between 1500 and 1922?

Objectives

By the end of this lesson you will be able to:

- choose which event is most significant
- explain why you think an event is historically significant

Getting you thinking

The image shows British troops in Dublin in 1916. They are there to put down an armed uprising against the government by Irish rebels. The rebels wanted to create an independent Ireland. This clearly was a major historical event which affected the growth of Britain. But was it the most significant event?

Events

1. **The Union of England and Wales (1536)**
   England and Wales are ruled together under the same law.

2. **The Union of Crowns between England and Scotland (1603)**
   James VI of Scotland becomes James I of England.

3. **The Act of Union between England and Scotland to form Great Britain (1707)**
   England and Scotland are united as one country.

4. **The Irish Rebellion of 1798 and the Act of Union (1800)**
   Following the defeat of the rebellion Britain and Ireland are united as one country.

5. **The Great Famine (1845–1849)**
   The failure of the Irish potato crops leads to the death of one million and emigration of another one and a half million people from Ireland.

6. **The Division of Ireland (1920–1922)**
   Ireland is divided in two. One part becomes the Irish Free State, a separate country. The other, Northern Ireland, stays part of the United Kingdom.

 ## Assessment task

Write a letter to the BBC, as an entry to a competition: 'What was the most significant event in the growth of Britain, 1500-1922?' Explain which event you have chosen, and why you think it is particularly significant.

Remember to plan your answer carefully.

To help you decide which event was the most significant you may wish to use the ideas below, developed by the historian Geoffrey Partington, about what makes an event historically significant:

- Did people living at the time think it was very important?
- Did it change things very much for people living at the time and make their lives different?
- Did it affect a lot of people's lives?
- Did it affect people's lives for a long time?
- Does it affect our lives today?

Soldiers man barricades in Dublin during the 1916 Easter Rising

Check your level

I can describe an event in some detail.

I can identify some of the consequences of the event.

I can organise the information to include ideas about significance, with evidence to support them.

I can include relevant dates and historical terms.

Level 4

I can use the information about the event to explain its historical significance.

I can show some links between the event and its consequences.

I can show links between the consequences of the event.

I can organise the information and ideas to answer the question.

I can give reasons for my ideas about historical significance, with evidence to support the reasons.

I can use relevant dates and historical terms correctly.

Level 5

I can examine and explain the reasons for and the consequences of the event and make links between them.

I know there are different historical interpretations of the significance of the event.

I can select and use relevant information to produce a structured answer.

I can use relevant dates and historical terms correctly.

Level 6

4 The beginnings of empire

Objectives

By the end of this unit you will be able to:

- describe how Britain began to create an empire overseas

Britain is a group of islands off the north-west coast of Europe. Its native language, English, is spoken all over the world. An important reason for this development was the growth of the British *Empire*, which continued from around 1700 to after the end of the First World War (1914–1918). How and why did Britain become interested in creating an empire across the world?

Empire: a group of countries ruled by one powerful country
Slave trade: the international trade in slaves from West Africa to the Americas

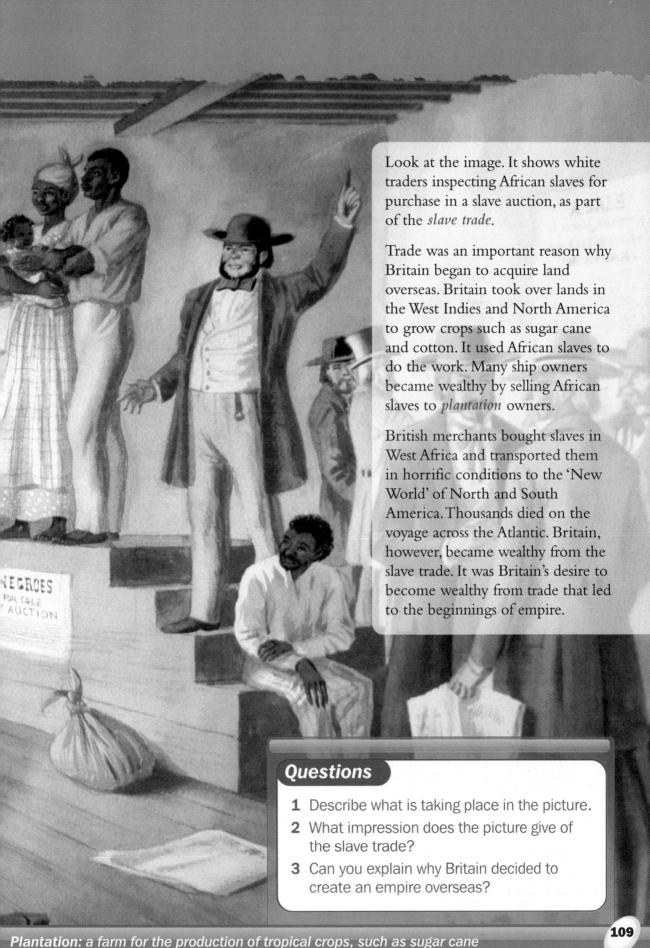

Look at the image. It shows white traders inspecting African slaves for purchase in a slave auction, as part of the *slave trade*.

Trade was an important reason why Britain began to acquire land overseas. Britain took over lands in the West Indies and North America to grow crops such as sugar cane and cotton. It used African slaves to do the work. Many ship owners became wealthy by selling African slaves to *plantation* owners.

British merchants bought slaves in West Africa and transported them in horrific conditions to the 'New World' of North and South America. Thousands died on the voyage across the Atlantic. Britain, however, became wealthy from the slave trade. It was Britain's desire to become wealthy from trade that led to the beginnings of empire.

Questions

1 Describe what is taking place in the picture.
2 What impression does the picture give of the slave trade?
3 Can you explain why Britain decided to create an empire overseas?

Plantation: a farm for the production of tropical crops, such as sugar cane

Britain and the world, 1700–1918

Objectives

By the end of the lesson you will be able to:

- organise events in Britain and the world, in the period 1700-1918, in chronological order
- explain the importance of different events and individuals in this period

Many important events and people shaped Britain in the period 1700-1918. Placing events in chronological order allows historians to have a more accurate view of the past.

Getting you thinking

Nelson's Column in Trafalgar Square, London, was built to celebrate Admiral Nelson's naval victory at the Battle of Trafalgar in 1805. Napoleon Bonaparte the *emperor* of France wanted to invade Britain. He could not launch an invasion due to the strength of the British Navy in the English Channel. Napoleon ordered the French Navy, under the command of Admiral Villeneuve, to sail towards the English Channel. On 21 October 1805, Nelson located Villeneuve and destroyed the French fleet at the Battle of Trafalgar. Nelson was killed on his ship, the HMS Victory. However, Napoleon did not invade Britain, and in 1815 was finally defeated at the Battle of Waterloo.

Not all important events are to do with war. Lady Mary Wortley introduced a smallpox inoculation into Britain in 1717. Immunity was gained by causing a mild form of the disease in healthy people, often by blowing powdered smallpox scabs up people's noses. A *vaccination* was fully developed in 1796 by Edward Jenner. Jenner's development of vaccinations resulted in the emergence of many other vaccines, such as today's swine flu vaccine. Today *smallpox* has nearly been wiped out as a disease.

Throughout the 19th century, various people attempted to build flying machines. On 17 December 1903, Wilbur and Orville Wright launched the first controlled, sustained and powered flight in the USA. From this point, flying developed rapidly, increasing travel and trade around the world.

Nelson's Column, London

Emperor: a man who rules an empire
Vaccination: introduction of a virus into a person to provide protection against diseases

Edward Jenner vaccinates a young boy against smallpox

There were many important events and individuals from 1700 to 1918. In 1914 one of the world's most destructive wars began, ending in 1918. In 1916 at the Battle of the Somme, the British Army suffered 70,000 *casualties* on the first day. However other events, such as the American Declaration of Independence in 1776, and the surrender of British Forces in 1781, resulted in the USA becoming the most powerful country in the world. The abolition of slavery within the British Empire in 1833 was a very important development, both for Britain and for other countries – including the USA, which fought a civil war over slavery thirty years later.

Now it's your turn

After reading the text, explain why you think the development of powered flights by Wilbur and Orville Wright was important.

Check your progress

I can describe different events from 1700 to 1918.
I can place these events in the correct chronological order.
I can explain the importance of events from 1700 to 1918.

Smallpox: a disease that causes fever and severe blisters
Casualty: a person killed or wounded in a battle

Britain: A trading nation

There were many reasons for Britain becoming an important trading nation in the period 1750–1900. Factors such as having a large navy encouraged trade.

Getting you thinking

Look at the pictures of tins on this page, and the designs on their lids.

- What did the tins contain, and when do you think they were made?
- What do they tell us about trade with other countries?
- What do they tell us about how the British liked to see themselves?

Britain in the eighteenth and nineteenth centuries had a large merchant navy and important ports, such as Bristol and Liverpool. Wealthy individuals provided finance to support trading voyages and find new trading opportunities. Increased wealth and a growing population in Britain also encouraged trade. British companies such as the East India Company, which operated from the 17th century to the early 19th century, helped to build the British Empire and create new trading links.

Customs duty/tariff: a tax placed on imports
Protectionism: protecting British companies by restricting other countries' right to trade

Most governments in the 18th century supported mercantilism. This was a trading system designed to protect British industry and control trade. Exports from Britain were sold to colonies within the empire, and imports such as sugar and tobacco were sent to Britain. This trade was protected through taxes, and through the army and navy. This policy was known as *protectionism,* meaning that only Britain could trade with British colonies. British governments placed *custom duties* or *tariffs* on goods coming into Britain. This encouraged people to buy cheaper British goods.

In the late 18th century and 19th century, however, more people were beginning to support *free trade,* as argued by Adam Smith in his book 'The Wealth of Nations'. He believed that customs duties and tariffs should be abolished to encourage trade. Smith believed this would increase profits for trading companies and for the nation as a whole. Adam Smith believed protectionism actually reduced trade.

British governments in the 1820s began to adopt a *laissez faire* position towards trade. Many customs duties and tariffs were removed by the mid-1850s. Support for the mercantile system had almost disappeared. As a result, British exports increased and secured Britain's position as the leading trading nation during the 19th century.

Trade was also encouraged by technological developments. Larger ships made of iron and powered by steam engines emerged. These ships brought cheaper raw materials to Britain, resulting in cheaper goods being made in British factories. This increased demand for such goods, which helped increase British trade in the 19th century.

Now it's your turn

Imagine you live in Britain in the early 19th century. Describe the type of exotic goods you might wish to buy, and how these could change your life. The items you are going to buy must have been available in the early 19th century – so no mobile phones or televisions, for example!

Check your progress

I can describe different causes of increased trade from 1700 to 1918.
I can explain why these causes are important.
I can explore links between different causes to explain why trade increased.

Free trade: removal of trading restrictions between countries
Laissez faire: A belief that the market should be allowed to run itself

The slave trade

Britain's participation in the slave trade caused great suffering. Yet successive British governments supported the slave trade.

Getting you thinking

- Why did people in 17th- and 18th-century Britain support *slavery*? Use the map below for possible ideas.

Britain supported the *trade triangle* in the 17th century and 18th century because it was very profitable. Britain sent goods to Africa to exchange for slaves. These slaves were then transported to the Americas and sold to *plantation* owners. Then raw materials such as sugar were sent back to Britain. Most slaves were bought from African and Arab slave traders.

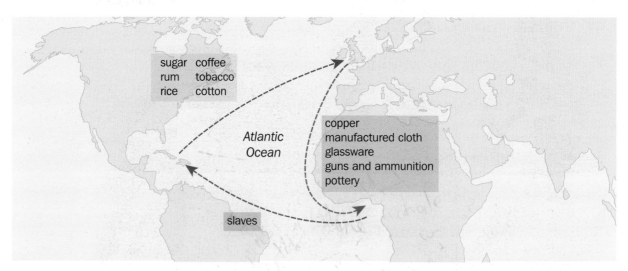

The trade triangle

In the period 1700–1807, approximately 12 million Africans were sent to the Americas in horrific conditions. The 'Brookes' slave ship carried 600 slaves when it was designed to carry only 451. Around 15 per cent of those sent died during the voyage. Many slaves died on the plantations through disease or harsh punishment.

However, huge profits drove the slave trade. Bristol and Liverpool grew due to slave trade profits. In the 1730s, the average voyage from Bristol picked up 170 slaves in Africa and made a large profit of £8,000. By 1771, there were 106 ships a year sailing from Liverpool, carrying a total of 282,000 slaves. By 1788, £200,000 worth of goods was being sent to Africa each year. Of this sum, £180,000 was used for buying slaves. In the 1790s Liverpool's slave trade accounted for 15 per cent of Britain's entire overseas trade.

Slavery: where people are bought and sold as property
Trade triangle: trading system based on the buying and selling of slaves in the 18th century

Many slaves worked on sugar and cotton plantations in the West Indies. Cotton was a vital raw material for Britain's growing industries. In 1770, a third of Manchester's *textiles* were exported to Africa and half to the West Indies. The slave trade provided many new jobs in Britain. In 1753 there were 120 sugar refineries in England. Many factories emerged in Liverpool to equip the slave ships. By 1774 there were fifteen rope factories in Liverpool.

Cheaper goods and foods improved people's living standards and diets. Sugar, for example, was added to foods such as bread and porridge. In 1700 British people ate four pounds of sugar each year, but by 1800 this had increased to 18 pounds. Many British families made enormous profits from the sugar plantations in the West Indies. Many people involved in the slave trade invested money in Britain. For example, James Watt's work with steam engines was partly financed by money from the West Indian slave trade.

Slaves were purchased from African and Arab slave traders in exchange for British goods

Now it's your turn

After reading the text, describe how a young child would feel being taken away from their family and being sold into slavery. You can work in pairs if you wish.

Check your progress

I can describe the different causes and consequences of the slave trade.
I can explain the importance of different causes and consequences.
I can explain why Britain supported the slave trade and the consequences of its support.

Plantation: a farm for the production of tropical crops, such as sugar cane
Textiles: industry making woven cloth

Colonial rule in the West Indies

Objectives

By the end of this lesson you will be able to:

- explain how the British kept control in the West Indies
- explain and develop different interpretations of British rule in the West Indies

The British used a variety of methods to control the West Indies. However, the slaves were never completely subdued and many rebelled against their owners and rulers.

Getting you thinking

- British *colonial rulers* used very violent methods to control their slaves. Why do you think this was?

Britain gradually exerted control over the West Indies in the 17th and 18th centuries. In 1655, the British took control of Jamaica from the Spanish, gaining more islands after their victories over the French in the Seven Years War (1756–1763) and the *Napoleonic Wars* (1799-1815). Britain was attracted by the sugar and rum that were produced in the islands. British companies encouraged settlers to emigrate to the West Indies. Each island had leaders and *assemblies* who answered to the British government. The plantation owners dominated political life in the islands.

A cartoon of colonial life in the West Indies

Colonial rulers: *people who ruled the West Indies for the British*
Napoleonic Wars: *fought by the British against Napoleon Bonaparte*

By the 1820s, 12 million people lived in the Americas. Two million were Europeans and the rest were slaves. Slave owners used violence to control and make slaves work harder. Many slaves died from the severe punishments they experienced. Slaves were organised to work from childhood to old age. Slave families were often split up when sold to other plantations for profits.

However, slaves still resisted the plantation owners. Some slaves ran away and established their own communities, becoming known as *Maroons*. They resisted by attacking plantations and setting slaves free. The British controlled the Maroons by granting them more freedom and even allowed them to own slaves.

In 1791 slaves rebelled on the French island of St Domingue and murdered white plantation owners. The British sent troops to crush the rebellion, but were defeated by a slave called Touissant L'Ouverture. The slaves declared their island independent, and renamed the island Haiti in 1804.

In 1831 a slave rebellion broke out in Jamaica, caused by a rumour that King William IV had granted slaves their freedom. The rebellion was led by Samuel Daddy Sharp. After four months the rebels were defeated and their leaders executed. However, the rebellion convinced the British prime minister, Earl Grey, that slavery should be completely abolished. Many people in Britain supported the abolition of slavery in the early 1830s. Slave owners were given £20 million in compensation for setting their slaves free.

Now it's your turn

After reading the text, identify different methods that the colonial rulers used to control the slaves. Then identify different ways in which the slaves resisted such control. Remember to explain your ideas with information from the text above.

Check your progress

I can describe how the British controlled the West Indies.
I can explain how slaves resisted the British.
I can discuss whether or not colonial rulers in the West Indies kept complete control over their slaves.

Assemblies: where people would meet to discuss and issue laws
Maroons: escaped slaves who established their own communities

Clarkson and the abolition of the slave trade

Objectives

By the end of this lesson you will be able to:

- explain the role of Clarkson in causing the abolition of the slave trade in 1807
- identify links between causes and explain the most important cause

In the late 18th century and early 19th century support for the *abolition* of slavery increased. Thomas Clarkson was an important supporter of abolition. He worked closely with abolitionists such as William Wilberforce and Granville Sharp.

Getting you thinking

This picture shows the interior of a slave ship and how slaves were loaded to maximise profits. Why do you think such diagrams increased support for the abolition of the slave trade?

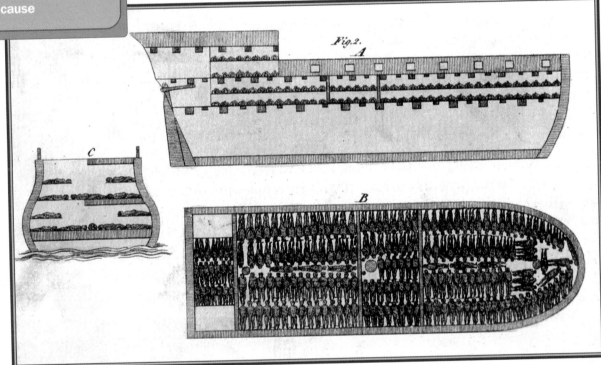

Plan of an eighteenth-century slave ship

Thomas Clarkson (1760–1846) produced such diagrams to show the horrors of slavery. Clarkson also interviewed 20,000 sailors and collected items used on slave ships such as thumb screws, iron handcuffs and branding irons, which revealed the cruelty of slavery. He also published pamphlets revealing the horrors of slavery. Clarkson worked closely with Granville Sharp. They established the Society for the Abolition of the Slave Trade, which was supported by important men such as William Wilberforce.

Abolition: the ending, in law, of a practice or tradition
Autobiography: a book written by a person about his or her own life

The book shown in the picture is the *autobiography* of Olaudah Equiano (1745-1797). Published in 1789, it became very popular. Equiano revealed the horrors of slavery through speeches and writing articles. He was a member of the organisation Sons of Africa, which consisted of 12 black men who campaigned against slavery.

In 1765 the campaigner Granville Sharp (1735-1813) took up the cause of a black slave called Jonathan Strong, who had been beaten and thrown onto the streets by his owner David Lisle. Sharp freed Strong by taking Lisle to court, arguing that Strong was now a free man. In 1768 the courts ruled in Strong's favour. The case gained national publicity and Sharp used this in his campaign against slavery. Sharp's most famous case focused on the 'Slave Ship Zong', where 133 sick slaves were thrown overboard. Equiano helped to bring this case to the attention of the British public.

William Wilberforce (1759–1833) supported Clarkson, Sharp and Equiano as a member of parliament. In 1807 the British government, with the support of Wilberforce, passed the Abolition of the Slave Trade Act. The act abolished the buying and selling of slaves in the British Empire but not the ownership of slaves. British sea captains caught carrying slaves were fined £100 for each slave they were carrying.

Now it's your turn

Imagine you are Thomas Clarkson and you are campaigning against the slave trade in the early 19th century. Write a speech that highlights the cruelty of slavery. You will also need to describe different methods people could use to campaign against slavery. Use the text above for ideas.

Check your progress

I can explain the role of Clarkson in causing the abolition of the slave trade in 1807.

I can explain how different individuals cooperated to end the slave trade.

I can explain links between causes of the abolition of the slave trade.

Wilberforce and the abolition of slavery in 1833

Objectives

By the end of this lesson you will be able to:

- explain the role of Wilberforce in causing the abolition of slavery in 1833
- describe the consequences of the abolition of slavery

William Wilberforce campaigned for the ending of the slave trade in 1807 and slavery in 1833. The abolition of slavery in 1833 had different consequences.

Getting you thinking

- What convinced Wilberforce to oppose slavery?

William Wilberforce campaigned against the slave trade, which was the buying and selling of slaves. He was a committed Christian and his religion inspired him to join the campaign. Wilberforce became the leader of the Clapham Sect, which consisted of devout Christians such as Thomas Clarkson and Granville Sharp. He first entered parliament in 1781, where he gave speeches against the slave trade. He also used his connections with powerful politicians such as Charles Fox to help end the slave trade. He introduced bills to the House of Commons, but his first bill, in 1791, was defeated. The slave trade was finally abolished by parliament in 1807.

William Wilberforce

However, people still owned slaves in the British Empire. The campaigner Thomas Buxton believed all forms of slavery should be ended. Wilberforce argued that slaves needed to be trained and educated before they could be freed. In 1823 Buxton convinced Wilberforce to change his views. Wilberforce retired from the House of Commons in 1825 and this reduced his influence. In 1833 parliament passed the Slavery Abolition Act, which gave all slaves in the British Empire their freedom.

Abolition of slavery had different consequences for Britain, slave owners and former slaves. One effect for Britain was that slave owners gained compensation from the British government. Twenty million pounds was put aside for compensation claims. The Bishop of Exeter had 665 slaves and received £12,700. The government made 40,000 separate compensation awards.

The 1833 Act only immediately freed slaves aged below six. Slaves over six were put into different categories according to their age, and after four years would be freed or paid a wage. By the 1840s, the 1833 Act had resulted in the freeing of the vast majority of slaves.

The abolition of slavery also had negative consequences. Plantation owners removed former slaves who were not prepared to work from their slave quarters. Slavery had failed to educate former slaves in how to cope in a market economy. Freedom often resulted in declining living standards and life expectancy for former slaves.

Profits of plantation owners in the West Indies also declined. The islands' economies depended on the sugar trade, and after 1833 plantation owners struggled to find workers. Many had to hire workers from Asia and Europe. The economic performance of the West Indies in the 19th century declined as compared to the 18th century.

Now it's your turn

1 Describe how slavery was abolished by Britain.
2 How important was Wilberforce in ending slavery? Give reasons for your answer.

Check your progress

I can explain how Wilberforce helped to bring about the abolition of slavery.

I can explain the importance of Wilberforce in the campaign.

I can describe different consequences of abolition.

Britain and India 1700–1918

Many events and people shaped India's relationship with Britain in the period 1700-1918. India became one of the most important areas of the British Empire.

Getting you thinking

- India was an important part of the British Empire. Why do you think India was so important to the British? The photograph might give you some ideas.

British control over India began with the collapse of the *Mughal Empire*. The last powerful Mughal emperor was Aurangzeb, who died in 1707. After his death, wars broke out amongst rival Indian princes. The British East India Company appointed Robert Clive to extend its power in India. The East India Company had its own troops. Clive gained territory for the company and he helped to defeat French

British ships at an Indian port in the late 19th century

Mughal Empire: An Indian empire which ruled India before the British took control
Viceroy: British rulers of India after 1857

forces and their allies. In 1757 Clive defeated Siraj ud Dowlah at the Battle of Plassey. This victory allowed the East India Company to dominate Bengal, one of the wealthiest areas in India. Britain was able to make huge profits from its Indian trade.

By the late 18th century and early 19th century, the British government gained more influence in India. In 1784 the India Act was passed by parliament to reduce the corruption of the East India Company. Governor generals were to be appointed directly by the British Crown. Lord William Bentinck, the governor general from 1828 to 1835, brought in unpopular laws. He made English the official language of India. He also banned the Indian tradition of 'suttee', where widows killed themselves when their husbands died.

The failed Indian Mutiny of 1857 changed how India was ruled. The British government created the British Indian Empire and ended East India Company rule. A *viceroy* replaced the governor general. The British did not directly govern all parts of India. Indian native states existed, which accepted British control over their relations with foreign countries. The old East India Company army was replaced by the British Indian Army. The changes prevented any more large-scale mutinies between 1857 and 1918. The period after 1857 is known as the 'golden age of the British *Raj*'.

However, many Indians still wanted to be free of their British rulers. In 1885 the Indian National Congress was established, and by World War One the congress was demanding more self-government for India. Many Indians fought for the British in World War One (1914–1918) and this increased Indian demands for self-government. During the war the British government promised that India could become a *dominion*. However, these promises were not kept when the war ended in 1918.

Now it's your turn

1 Create a timeline showing different events affecting British rule in India, 1700–1918.
2 What was the most important event in this period?

Check your progress

I can explain the impact of events on Britain and India from 1700 to 1918.
I can place these events in the correct chronological order.
I can explain the importance of these events.

Raj: refers to British rule in India from 1858 to 1947
Dominion: a country within the British Empire, but with some independence

The Indian Mutiny, 1857

Objectives

By the end of the lesson you will be able to:

- explain the causes of the revolt
- decide who was more brutal during the mutiny

The Indian Mutiny of 1857 was the closest the British came to losing control over India in the 19th century. During the mutiny both the British and the Indian rebels committed very violent and cruel acts.

Getting you thinking

- Can you decide who was more brutal during the mutiny?

The cartoon below, from *Punch* magazine, wants to show that British forces were fighting for justice during the Indian Mutiny, which began in May 1857. The final spark that started the revolt was when *sepoys* in the Indian army refused to bite cartridges before loading them into their Enfield Rifles. Most Sepoys were either Muslims or Hindus. They believed the cartridges had cow and pig grease in them. In the Hindu religion, cows are sacred animals. Muslims believe that pigs are unclean and should not be eaten. Many Indians were also unhappy that the British were ending some of their traditions, such as banning *suttee* and making English the official language of India.

JUSTICE.

Cartoon of 'The Sepoy Mutiny' in *Punch* magazine, 1857

Sepoys: Indian troops who served in the British Army

The revolt began in Meerut near Delhi in northern India. Eighty-five sepoys refused to use the cartridges. They were arrested and chained together and sentenced to ten years' hard labour. This harsh punishment caused more sepoys to rebel in Meerut and they executed their British officers. The revolt spread across northern India. The rebels captured Indian towns such as Delhi. One of the most violent events took place in Cawnpore. General Wheeler, 300 soldiers and their families were besieged by rebel forces led by Nana Sahib. In June 1857, the British surrendered and Sahib told them they could leave by the river. However, he broke the agreement and attacked the soldiers. He also ordered the execution of the women and children, many of whom had their throats cut.

British forces under the leadership of General Havelock reached Cawnpore and discovered the massacre. Havelock ordered Colonel Neil to punish captured Indian rebels. Colonel Neil did not hold trials. He ordered that the Muslim prisoners be forced to eat pork and the Hindus be forced to eat beef. The prisoners were also forced to lick up the blood of their victims. After being humiliated the prisoners were then hanged.

It took over a year for British soldiers, with the support of loyal *Sikh* troops, to crush the revolt. Thousands were executed for participating in the revolt. The British viewed the revolt as led by people who failed to see the benefits of the British Empire. Many Indians joined the revolt because they believed they were defending their religion and traditions against their oppressive British rulers.

Now it's your turn

1 Can you give two reasons why the Indian mutiny began in 1857?
2 How did the Indian rebels treat their enemies and how did the British punish the rebels?
3 Who do you think was worse in their actions: the Indian rebels or the British? Give reasons for your answer.

Check your progress

I can explain some of the key events of the mutiny.
I can describe some reasons why the mutiny happened.
I can say whether the British or rebels were more brutal during the rebellion, and give reasons.

British rule in India

Objectives

By the end of this lesson you will be able to:

- explain how the British ruled India from 1858 to 1918
- explain why people differed in their views about the success of British rule

The rule of the East India Company was ended in 1857. After 1858 the British used different methods to rule India. British rule had both successes and failures in the period 1858–1918.

Getting you thinking

- Why do you think many Indians found the British to be *arrogant* rulers?

After 1857, the British government ruled India through viceroys. They governed India with about 3,000 British officials. India had a population of around 300 million. In 1877, Queen Victoria became the 'Empress of India'. In the period 1858–1918 the British successfully prevented large-scale mutinies.

The role of the Indian Army was to defend the North-West Frontier against a Russian invasion through Afghanistan, and to maintain security within India. By 1914, the Indian Army numbered 150,000 men. Recruitment was voluntary. During World War One (1914–1918) about 1.3 million Indians served in the British India Army, which contributed to victory in 1918. The British government sent regiments from the United Kingdom to serve in India. They were known as the British Army in India.

Many Indians believed British rule had failed them. They were often treated as inferiors and regarded their British rulers as arrogant. Many British officials ignored Indian customs and traditions, and believed the English race and culture was superior. General Mayo, the Viceroy of India from 1869 to 1872, stated: 'We are all British gentlemen engaged in the magnificent work of governing an inferior race.' In 1914 only 5 per cent of *administrators* in British India were Indian. Many Indian professionals, such as lawyers, felt excluded.

In the late 19th century more Indians wanted greater self-government but were largely ignored by the British. Lord Curzon, who was Viceroy of India from 1898 to 1905, disliked the Indian National Congress and its support for more self-government. He was determined to strengthen British rule in India. Curzon improved road and rail links in India and encouraged British investment within India. He decided to divide the state of Bengal, to make the governing of this large and powerful area of India more efficient. However, this decision resulted in widespread Indian protests led by the Congress. Indians wanted to protect the distinct identity of

Arrogant: having an exaggerated opinion of your own importance
Administrator: a person who helps run a country or organisation

The British viceroy and his wife, on a tiger hunt

Bengal, which numbered 78 million people. One Indian leader, Tilak, supported more violent confrontation with the British, but the majority of Indians preferred more peaceful methods.

In 1905 a new Liberal government came to power in Britain. Lord Curzon was replaced by the more moderate Lord Minto. However, Minto was not prepared to allow India more self government. In 1910 the new viceroy, Lord Hardinge, developed closer links with Congress members such as Gokhale. Liberal policies in India from 1905 to 1914 successfully reduced tensions. When World War One ended in 1918, however, the British did not allow India to become a dominion.

Now it's your turn

1 What different methods did the British use to rule India?
2 Were the methods they used successful?

Check your progress

I can explain how the British ruled India.
I can explain the successes of British rule.
I can explain both the successes and failures of British rule.

127

Britain and North America, 1607–1800

Objectives

By the end of this lesson you will be able to:

- describe the events which led to the development of British rule in North America
- understand the chronological order of these events and explain their importance
- make links between events

Getting you thinking

Look at the picture. It shows the first European settlers, known as the 'Pilgrim Fathers', leaving England for America in the early 17th century. This was part of a move by some European countries to set up colonies. Both Britain and France wanted to acquire land, develop trade and spread Christianity. This caused conflict between the two countries. By the end of the 18th century Britain had defeated France and created a large colonial empire. How did British acquire so much land in America?

Britain in North America

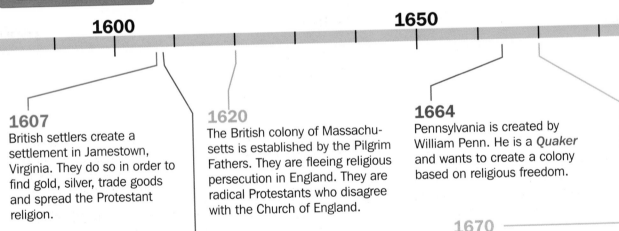

1600

1650

1607
British settlers create a settlement in Jamestown, Virginia. They do so in order to find gold, silver, trade goods and spread the Protestant religion.

1620
The British colony of Massachusetts is established by the Pilgrim Fathers. They are fleeing religious persecution in England. They are radical Protestants who disagree with the Church of England.

1664
Pennsylvania is created by William Penn. He is a *Quaker* and wants to create a colony based on religious freedom.

1608
French create the town of Quebec, in modern-day Canada as a *trading post* and a base to spread the Catholic religion.

1670
Britain creates the Hudson's Bay Company to develop trade with Canada. The company is a rival of French traders in Canada.

Now it's your turn

1 Identify two reasons why British colonies were created in North America.
2 What links can you make between the reasons why Britain and France went to war in North America?
3 What do you regard as the most important event in the development of British rule in North America? Give a reason to explain your answer.

Trading post: a place used for trading goods
Quakers: a Protestant religious group separate from the Church of England

The Pilgrim Fathers leaving England for America

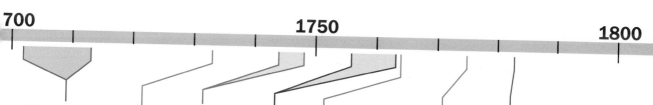

700 · · · · · **1750** · · · · · **1800**

1702–13
Queen Anne's War between Britain and France. The war is fought over trade and is part of a war between the two countries in Europe.

1744–48
War resumes with France in King George's War. The war is fought over trade and land and problems in Europe.

1764
Britain begins to tax the British colonies in North America to help pay for Britain's North American army. This leads to protests by colonists against taxation.

1783
Britain is forced to give independence to the 13 colonies, which become the United States.

1775
British colonists in the 13 Colonies of the modern-day eastern United States revolt against British rule. It is the start of the American War of Independence.

1733
The British colony of Georgia is created. Britain now has 13 colonies in eastern North America and more colonies in Canada.

1756–63
Britain defeats France in the French and Indian War. The war is fought over trade and land, and is part of a worldwide war between the two countries. Britain wins and now dominates all of eastern North America.

Check your progress

I can describe events in the development of Britain's rule in North America from 1600 to 1800.
I can make connections between events.
I can explain the importance of these events.

Causes of the American War of Independence

Objectives

By the end of this lesson you will be able to:

- give reasons why the American War of Independence began
- explain the causes of the war and find links between them

No taxation without representation!

In 1763 Britain had won a great victory over France in the French and Indian War. All of France's colonies in North America now became part of Britain's empire. Yet within 12 years, 13 of Britain's American colonies rose in revolt against British rule. The picture shows one of the acts of rebellion. So, why did such a change take place?

Getting you thinking

1763 was a year of victory for Britain and the American colonists. The French threat in North America had come to an end. However, Britain's victory created problems that eventually led to war.

Britain had gained large amounts of land from France, but in 1763 Britain would not allow American colonists to enter these new lands. This caused resentment among the colonists who wanted to expand westwards.

The 'Boston Tea Party' of 1773

Repeal: to cancel an act of parliament

The war against France had cost a lot of money. So did the maintenance of a British army in North America. So the British government expected the colonists to pay towards these costs. The government in Britain passed acts of parliament to raise money, such as the Stamp Act of 1765. This placed a tax on newspapers and official documents. This was done without consulting the colonists. The Stamp Act caused widespread rioting in America and demands for repeal. In 1766 the king, George III, *repealed* the act. This gave the signal to the colonists that opposition to British laws could be successful.

In 1770 rioters opposed taxes on trade. In Boston, *New England*, troops shot and killed five rioters.

In 1773 the government passed the Tea Act, which lowered tax on British tea, making it cheaper than American tea. In Boston Harbour, colonists dressed as Native Americans boarded tea ships and threw the British tea into the harbour. The incident became known as the 'Boston Tea Party'.

In 1774 Britain's government allowed the former French colony of Quebec to give the Catholic Church a special position. This infuriated the Protestant population of Britain's 13 colonies.

The colonists then met together in an assembly called the Continental Congress. The assembly aimed to oppose British laws. They claimed that no taxation should be made in the 13 colonies without the support of the colonists. 'No Taxation without representation' became the slogan of colonial opposition to Britain's rule in North America.

In the following year, 1775, British troops in New England attempted to take guns and ammunition away from the colonists. At Lexington and Concord, troops and colonists clashed. The American War of Independence had begun.

Now it's your turn APP

1 Can you identify three reasons why the American War of Independence took place?
2 What do you regard as the most important reason for the outbreak of the American War of Independence? Give reasons to support your answer.
3 Can you find links between the causes of the war? Try to connect the causes that are linked with:
   • taxation
   • trade
   • religion

Check your progress

⋆ I can describe events that led to the outbreak of war.
⋆⋆ I can show how different causes linked together leading to war.
⋆⋆⋆ I can identify which causes are more or less important.

New England: the 13 northern colonies

Britain loses the war

In the American War of Independence, Britain had the world's best navy and one of its largest armies. The American colonists were a ramshackle band of farmers and townspeople. However, the Americans won. The picture shows the final surrender of Britain at Yorktown. How could the world's greatest empire lose?

Getting you thinking

Britain had to fight a war over 3,000 miles from Britain. It took over two months to sail from Britain to the 13 colonies.

Many of the 13 colonies were heavily wooded, divided by rivers and mountains. This was very difficult country for the British army to fight in.

The colonists were formed into an army by George Washington. Washington avoided major battles so as to prolong the war, which would make the British give up.

British troops were led by poor commanders. General Burgoyne, who attempted to split New England from the rest of the colonies, was surrounded by the Americans at Saratoga. He was forced to surrender his whole army. This was the first major victory for the colonists.

Objectives

By the end of this lesson you will be able to:

- describe the main events of the American War of Independence
- explain the importance of different events in the American War of Independence

The leader of the British Army, General Cornwallis, surrenders at Yorktown

The Battle of Saratoga convinced the British prime minister, Lord North, that the war could not be won. It also persuaded France to join the American colonists in the war against Britain.

Many people in Britain supported the American colonists' demand for 'no taxation without representation'.

France, Spain and Holland joined the war on the American side from 1778. They had modern armies and large navies. Britain had to fight a war in the colonies, Europe, the West Indies and India.

In 1779 the British navy lost control of the North Atlantic ocean. This was the only time Britain lost control of this area in the entire 18th century.

American and French troops forced a British army under Lord Cornwallis to surrender at the costal town of Yorktown. Cornwallis could not pull his army out because the French navy controlled the sea off the coast of North America.

Timeline of the War

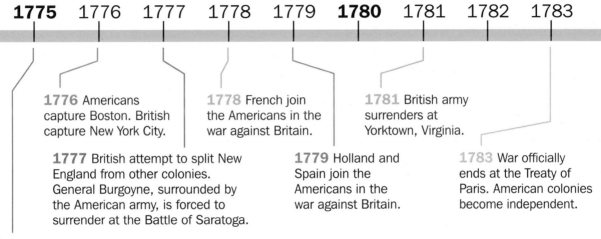

1775 1776 1777 1778 1779 **1780** 1781 1782 1783

1776 Americans capture Boston. British capture New York City.

1778 French join the Americans in the war against Britain.

1781 British army surrenders at Yorktown, Virginia.

1777 British attempt to split New England from other colonies. General Burgoyne, surrounded by the American army, is forced to surrender at the Battle of Saratoga.

1779 Holland and Spain join the Americans in the war against Britain.

1783 War officially ends at the Treaty of Paris. American colonies become independent.

1775 British troops and colonists clash at Lexington and Concord. The war begins. British defeat Americans at Boston in Battle of Bunker Hill.

Now it's your turn

1 Can you identify three problems Britain faced when fighting the American War of Independence?
2 Why do you think the Americans won the war?
3 A turning point is an important moment that changes the course of historical events. What do you regard as the turning point of the American War of Independence? Give reasons for your answer.

Check your progress

★ I can describe events in the American War of Independence.

★ ★ I can explain reasons why the Americans won the war.

★ ★ ★ I can explain the meaning of the historical term 'turning point'.

George Washington: The man who created the United States?

Objectives

By the end of this lesson you will be able to:

- describe some of the qualities of Washington as a person
- give reasons why Washington was a significant person in history

The picture shows a painting of George Washington as leader of the American troops in the War of Independence. In 1789 Washington became the first president of the United States. The present-day capital of the USA, Washington D.C., is named after him. So is one of the 50 states. So how important was George Washington to the creation of the United States?

WASHINGTON. CROSSING THE DELAWARE.

Washington crossing the Delaware river: this was a surprise attack that helped win the war for the American side

Now it's your turn

Your task is to produce a cartoon strip summary of George Washington's life and work. If you prefer you could write the brief for an artist to draw the illustrations rather than do them yourself. Make sure you pick out events that suggest that he was a significant person in the history of the USA.

Congress: the parliament of the United States
Constitutional Convention: a meeting to decide how the country would be governed

Getting you thinking

Six feet two inches tall and as straight as an Indian. In the spring of 1775 he took command of an army that was no more than a group of undisciplined farmers.

Source 1 *A description of Washington in 1775 (From The American Revolution by Esmond Wright)*

Washington knew that for the Americans to succeed they had only to defend themselves against the British. The British faced the heavier burden of sending troops 3,000 miles to crush the rebellion. If the British were unsuccessful and decided to go home, the Americans would have their independence. In order to fight a defensive war, Washington knew that at minimum his army had to survive. So Washington was careful to never allow his army to be trapped where there was no retreat possible. He always recognised when to use retreat against overwhelming odds so his army could survive to fight another day.

Source 2 *Washington in the War of Independence*

'First in war, first in peace, and first in the hearts of his countrymen.' These words were included in the memorial to George Washington by the US Congress at the time of his death. While Americans today recognise Washington as the first president, many do not realise his importance as a military leader. After all, had it not been for Washington's success in the American War of Independence, there would not have been a first president of the United States.

Source 3 *George Washington as military leader*

George Washington in many ways was, and remains, the model of what it means to be an American citizen. He possessed many of the characteristics. These were:
1. self-restraint
2. self-assertion
3. self-reliance

Source 5 *A view of Washington by James Madison, 4th President of the USA*

In 1787, Washington led the Virginia delegation to the Constitutional Convention in Philadelphia. He was unanimously elected presiding officer. His presence gave prestige to the meetings although he made few direct contributions. After the new Constitution was approved by the 13 states, he was unanimously elected president in 1789.

Source 4 *A Description of Washington at the Constitutional Convention*

Sources 2, 3 and 4 are from a US history website on George Washington

Check your progress

I can describe reasons why Washington is seen as an important person.
I can explain why Washington is seen as a significant person in American history.
I can explain what makes a person significant in history.

Unanimous: with everyone in agreement

A country without a king: The United States

The illustration shows George Washington as the first president of the United States. Unlike the vast majority of European states at the time, the USA decided to become a republic – a country without a king.

Getting you thinking

In 1787, representatives from each of the 13 states met in the hot, humid summer of Philadelphia. Each wanted to keep control of its own affairs as much as possible. However, all the states realised they had to work together to prevent attack from other countries and to encourage trade. They came together to produce a constitution for a new state. These would be the rules which decided how political power was divided.

The 13 states were of different sizes. Some were large with big populations, such as Virginia. Others were small, such as Rhode Island. Each had its own way of organising its government.

The 13 states had revolted against Britain because they feared *tyranny*. If they were to create their own new country they wanted to prevent any one person or organisation having complete power. If any agreement was to take place, it would involve compromise by all the states.

George Washington as president in 1789

Tyranny: oppressive rule by one person or group

Who was to be the chairman of this mixed gathering of states?

The states chose George Washington. He had been the general who had led the states to victory over Britain.

How to avoid tyranny?

The representatives at Philadelphia decided to divide political power between the states and a national government. The national government had control over foreign affairs, national defence and trade between the states. Everything else such as law and order and education was controlled by individual states.

In the national government, political power was divided between an elected president, a parliament and a court of law. No one part of government could act alone. It had to get the support of the other two parts of the national government. This was called the separation of power.

What made the United States different from most European countries was the decision not to have a monarch. Instead it became a *republic*. It was to have an elected president chosen for a four-year period of office. George Washington was chosen as the first president and took office in 1789.

The US system of government
President
- elected every four years
- head of armed forces
- responsible for foreign policy

Laws were made by Congress, consisting of two houses, the Senate and the House of Representatives.

Senate
- each state, whether large or small, had two senators
- elected new senators every 6 years

House of Representatives
- states had seats based on their population, so large states had more representatives

Laws passed by Congress would then be reviewed by the Supreme Court.

Supreme Court
- members chosen for life
- interpreted the constitution
- could decide whether or not the president or Congress acted lawfully

Now it's your turn
1 What problems faced the representatives at Philadelphia?
2 How did the representatives attempt to prevent tyranny?
3 How did the national government:
- split political power between the President, Congress and the Supreme Court?
- please both large and small states?

Check your progress
I can describe how the government of the United States was formed.
I can explain how political power was divided.
I can explain how the government attempted to avoid tyranny.

Republic: government without a monarch

The beginnings of empire

In unit 3 you looked at which historical events were significant. You are now going to explore one of the most significant events in the history of the British empire during the nineteenth century.

Assessment task: the slave trade

Your task is to produce a piece of written work on why the slave trade was abolished.

You will need to do the following:
- explain why the slave trade was abolished
- identify links between reasons for the end of the slave trade
- show that there are different interpretations for why historical events took place
- use formal language in your answer

Objectives

By the end of this lesson you will be able to:
- make a judgement about the level of a piece of work
- suggest improvements to a piece of work

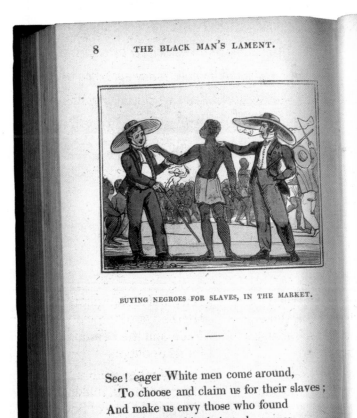

8   THE BLACK MAN'S LAMENT.   THE BLACK MAN'S LAMENT.   9

BUYING NEGROES FOR SLAVES, IN THE MARKET.   STANDING IN LINES, WITH THE DRIVER BEHIND.

See! eager White men come around,
    To choose and claim us for their slaves;
And make us envy those who found
    In the dark ship their early graves:

They bid black men and women stand
    In lines, the drivers in the rear:
Poor Negroes hold a *hoe* in hand,
    But they the wicked cart-whip bear.

Pages from 'The Black Man's Lament', an anti-slavery poem written by Amelia Opie

Two students were asked to carry out the same task you have been set.
Here are parts of their answers.

Erin's answer:

The slave trade was abolished because people thought it was inhuman. Black people from Africa were captured and forced into crowded ships.

Most were forced to travel across the Atlantic ocean to America in chains. En route many died. When they arrived in the New World they were sold and forced to work for their white masters for no pay.

This trade was opposed by many Christians who saw it as wrong for one person to own another. In 1807 Britain decided to end the trade.

Joshua's answer

The slave trade was abolished by the British government in 1807. This was because many people had campaigned to end the trade. An important person was Thomas Clarkson. He explained how British ships were packed with African slaves in their journey across the Atlantic ocean. Many slaves were chained and tortured on the journey. Clarkson produced pamphlets to show this evil trade across Britain.

He was helped by Granville Sharp who set up the Society for the Abolition of the Slave Trade.

Their campaign was helped by a former slave, Equiano. He gave many speeches and also wrote about how bad slavery was. His own life story was published as a book in 1789.

These campaigns helped force Britain's parliament to ban the slave trade.

1 What level have Joshua and Erin reached in their answers? Use the table to help you decide.
2 Look at Erin's answer. What advice could you give her to improve her answer?
3 Now mark your own answer. What level did you reach? How can you improve your work?

Check your level

I can include knowledge of the slave trade and the campaign for its abolition.	I can include detailed knowledge of the slave trade and the campaign for its abolition.	I can include detailed knowledge of the slave trade and the campaign for its abolition.
I can give the work a clear structure.	I can give the work a clear structure and use appropriate language.	I can give the work a clear structure, making appropriate use of dates and historical terms.
I can give reasons why events took place.	I can give detailed reasons why events took place.	I can provide links between the reasons why events took place.
Level 4	Level 5	Level 6

Objectives

By the end of this unit you will be able to:

- make a judgement on why the empire was important in British history

It might be hard to believe now that 100 years ago Britain had the world's greatest empire. The British flag flew over large parts of Africa, Asia, Australasia and the Americas. One third of the world's population in 1900 regarded Britain's Queen Victoria as their ruler.

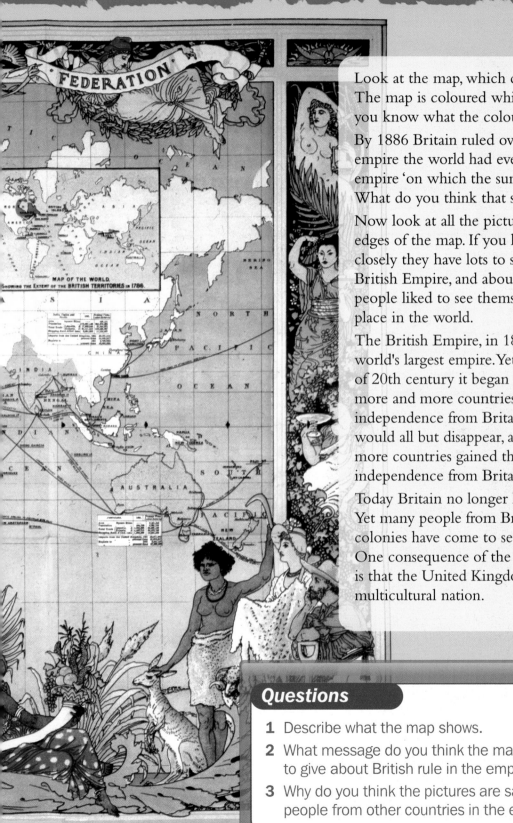

Look at the map, which dates from 1886. The map is coloured white and pink; do you know what the colours are showing?

By 1886 Britain ruled over the largest empire the world had ever seen, an empire 'on which the sun never sets'. What do you think that saying means?

Now look at all the pictures around the edges of the map. If you look at them closely they have lots to say about the British Empire, and about the way British people liked to see themselves and their place in the world.

The British Empire, in 1886, was the world's largest empire. Yet by the middle of 20th century it began to shrink as more and more countries gained their independence from Britain. Eventually, it would all but disappear, as more and more countries gained their independence from Britain.

Today Britain no longer has an empire. Yet many people from Britain's former colonies have come to settle in Britain. One consequence of the British Empire is that the United Kingdom is now a multicultural nation.

Questions

1 Describe what the map shows.
2 What message do you think the map is trying to give about British rule in the empire?
3 Why do you think the pictures are saying about people from other countries in the empire?

The lion's share: the British Empire in 1918

Getting you thinking

The picture below is the cover of an annual from 1913, showing Britain as a roaring lion. In 1918 Britain had the world's largest empire, covering a quarter of the world's surface. It also contained a third of the entire world's population. How did a small country off the coast of Europe come to possess the world's greatest empire?

Britain acquired a large empire for a variety of reasons.

Trade

Britain wanted raw materials for its manufacturers and new markets for British goods:

- India from 1612 until the end of 19th century provided goods such as cotton and a place to sell British goods.
- The islands of the West Indies produced sugar after the 1660s.
- Hong Kong, a British colony, began to trade with China in 1842.
- South Africa provided gold from the 1880s.
- Canada produced wheat.
- Until the abolition of the slave trade in 1807, slaves for the West Indies plantations came from Gambia and Ghana in west Africa.

Cover of the *Standard of Empire Annual 1912–1913*

Protection of trade routes

Britain occupied other places to protect its sea routes, to ensure trade could continue safely. The British established colonies in:

- Singapore (1815)
- Cape of Good Hope (1806)
- Falkland Islands (1833)

Naval bases

Britain had the world's greatest navy after the 18th century. It required naval bases around the world. When coal became the major fuel for naval vessels, these bases also acted as coaling stations:

- Gibraltar (1713)
- Malta (1815)
- Singapore (1815)
- Labuan Island off Borneo (1842)

Victory in war

Britain won many wars from the 18th century to 1918. As the victor, Britain was able to acquire territory from the defeated countries:

- Quebec in Canada from France (1763)
- Tanganyika in East Africa from Germany (1918)

Land for settlement

Many British people wanted to start new lives overseas. Parts of the British Empire provided new lands for these settlers:

- Australia from 1788
- Canada in the 19th century
- New Zealand in the 1840s

Protecting British lands in India

India was regarded as the most important part of the British Empire. It was called 'the jewel in the crown of the Empire'. To protect India from attack, Britain acquired the following territories:

- the region of present-day Pakistan in the 1840s
- Myanmar (Burma) in the 1880s

Spreading the Christian religion

British missionaries went overseas to spread the Christian religion to non-Christian people:

- Uganda in the 1890s

Now it's your turn

1 What reasons can you give for Britain acquiring an overseas empire?
2 Can you show how any of the reasons why Britain acquired an empire are linked? Give reasons to support your answer.
3 Draw a graph and place on it, in chronological order, the colonies mentioned above.
4 What do you think was the period of greatest expansion of the British Empire?

Check your progress

I can describe how Britain expanded its empire.
I can explain the chronological development of the British Empire.
I can explain links between reasons for the growth of empire.

Impact of the empire on Britain

Objectives

At the end of the lesson you will be able to:

- describe the different ways the empire affected Britain
- explain the impact of the empire on life and work in Britain

Victoria's Diamond Jubilee, London, 1897

Getting you thinking

The photograph shows Queen Victoria's Diamond Jubilee in 1897. She had been Britain's queen for 60 years. The occasion was used to celebrate Britain's empire. The empire had a major impact on life and work in Britain. In school classrooms across Britain in 1900, maps of the world showed Britain's vast empire, coloured pink. Pride in the empire was encouraged; troops from across the empire marched through London in celebrations. In schools children dressed up as peoples of the empire.

- How did the empire affect life and work in Britain?

Refrigerated ships: ships with a cold store that preserved foodstuffs

Helping industry

The empire provided Britain with raw materials for the expansion of industry in the 19th century. Cotton from India and Egypt was used in the cotton towns of Lancashire to make cotton cloth that was sold around the world. Flax from India was used as the raw material for Northern Ireland's linen industry, centred in Belfast. Wool from Australia and New Zealand was used in the Yorkshire woollen cloth industry in the area around Leeds and Bradford.

Changing Britain's diet

Many parts of the empire produced cheap food for Britain's workforce. Wheat from Canada helped provide cheap bread. When *refrigerated ships* were developed in the 1880s, lamb and butter were imported from New Zealand, and meat from Australia. The cost of buying food for most workers actually dropped during the second half of the 19th century.

Opportunities abroad?

Emigration to many parts of the empire allowed people to leave a life of poverty in the British Isles. Irish farmers fled famine to go to places like Canada and Australia. British workers fled the harsh life in factories for new lives in Australia, Canada and New Zealand.

Emigration also had a less pleasant side. Until the 1840s convicts were sent to places like Australia. Orphans in workhouses were also sent to parts of the empire to reduce the costs of welfare.

Encouragement of banking

The empire created many opportunities to trade and create businesses abroad. This led to the creation of many banks in the City of London, which provided loans to companies. By 1900 London was the world's greatest centre for banking. Much of this was due to the empire.

The world's greatest navy

In order to protect and defend the empire, Britain built the world's greatest navy. This encouraged shipbuilding in towns such as Newcastle, Barrow in Furness and east London. It also led to the creation of naval bases at Plymouth, Portsmouth and Chatham.

Now it's your turn

1 How did the growth of empire affect working life in Britain?
2 What do you regard as the most important impact of empire on Britain? Give reasons to support your answer.

Extension work

Do you think the people who celebrated Queen Victoria's 60 years on the throne should have felt pride in Britain's empire?

Check your progress

I can describe some different ways the empire affected Britain.
I can describe some positive aspects of the empire for life in Britain.
I can suggest ways in which the consequences of the empire are still felt today.

Life under the British Empire

By the end of the First World War, Britain's empire stretched across the world. Britain had colonies on every continent. Britain regarded its empire with pride.

- But how was life under British rule for the peoples of the empire?

Getting you thinking

Britain liked to think that life in its empire was orderly and civilised. Many Britons thought they were involved in bringing modern developments to the diverse peoples under its rule. However, life under the British flag was not always so rosy!

Who were the rulers?

Local non-British people had little opportunity to take part in government. In fact, by the time of World War One (1914–1918), the empire was divided into white and non-white areas. Colonies with large white populations were given the chance to rule themselves within the empire. These included Canada, Australia, New Zealand and South Africa. However, these colonies also contained non-white populations. These were treated as second-class citizens. They could not vote or take part in government.

Colonies without large white populations were ruled directly from London. British officials were sent to India, Africa and the West Indies to govern the local populations.

Bringing civilisation?

Being part of the British Empire clearly brought some benefits to the governed. Britain built the railway system in India, which transformed internal travel. The introduction of postal services, telegraph and telephone systems brought modern communications to much of the empire. The use of English as the empire's 'universal' language allowed people from different corners of the empire to talk to each other.

Exploiting the peoples of the Empire?

Many of the non-white peoples of the empire suffered. Native Americans in Canada and *Maoris* in New Zealand lost lands to white settlers. The *Aborigines* of Australia saw an attempt to destroy their way of life.

Many people in the empire were forced to work for British-owned companies in poor working and living conditions. The worst exploitation was in the West Indies, where slavery of black people was allowed until 1833. After the end of slavery, black West Indians still worked for low pay in plantations.

In India, many people worked in poor conditions producing cotton for Britain.

Maoris: the native people of New Zealand
Aborigines: the original inhabitants of Australia

A British outpost in Polynesia, 1792

The natives fight back!

By 1918, opposition to British rule began to grow. In India, western-educated Indians formed the Indian National Congress to demand self-government for Indians within the empire. In Ireland nationalists also wanted the same, known as Home Rule. In South Africa many Dutch speakers revolted against British rule. Also in South Africa, just before World War One, black people formed the African National Congress to campaign for *civil rights*.

Now it's your turn

1   How different was life in the empire for white and non-white peoples before 1918?
2   In what ways did some people in the empire show their disapproval of British rule?
3   Draw up a list of benefits and problems of living under British rule.
4   What do you regard as the most significant impacts of the empire on those who were governed?

Check your progress

I can explain how the empire affected those who were governed.
I can describe positive and negative aspects of the empire for non-white peoples.
I can give examples of resistance to the British empire before 1918.

Civil rights: rights including the vote and free speech

The empire and trade

The photograph shows British docks at the end of Queen Victoria's reign.

Getting you thinking

At that time Britain was the world's greatest trading nation. 75 per cent of merchant ships were British-owned. Britain had the world's biggest economy. It was known as the 'workshop of the world'. British ports exported all over the globe. How important was the empire in this British trade? What was the impact of trade on Britain's *colonies*?

The picture below shows a busy scene in London's docks in the early 20th century. Goods from all over Britain were exported abroad. These included cotton and woollen cloth, coal, iron and steel, and machines of all types. Britain had also been involved in the trade in people. Up to 1807 Britain was a major trader in slaves from Africa to the Americas. From the middle of the 19th century, millions left Britain for new lives overseas.

Objectives

By the end of the lesson you will be able to:

- describe the main features of British trade in the early 20th century
- use and interpret statistical information
- describe the impact of trade with the Empire on Britain

Colony: an overseas territory in an empire
Investments: the use of money to buy companies

Table 1: The destination of British goods in 1912

Destination	Value of exports
Western Europe	205
Rest of Europe	481
USA	119
Canada	82
India	199

The numbers are in millions of £s
From 'A History of Economic Change in England 1880-1939' by RS Sayers, 1967

Table 2: British *investments* abroad in 1912

British Empire	46
South America	22
USA	19
Europe	6

The numbers are percentages of total British investment overseas.
From 'The Age of Empire' by E J Hosbawm, 1987

Britain traded with almost every country on earth. Yet in Britain many politicians claimed that Britain still needed a large empire to maintain its trade. As Britain developed into the world's first industrial country, it required raw materials for its growing factories. These included cotton, which came from the United States, Egypt and India. From 1850 Britain produced most of the world's cotton cloth even though cotton did not grow in Britain.

As a major producer of manufactured goods, Britain needed people to buy its products. The empire was seen as a major purchaser of these goods. The cotton factories of the Manchester area provided the clothing for much of British India.

But was this really true? Study the tables above, of statistics about British overseas trade.

Now it's your turn

1 Which parts of the world were most important for British trade in 1912?
2 Study tables 1 and 2. How important were countries in the empire for British exports and investment abroad?

Extension work

Write a series of letters between two British politicians in 1900, on the importance of the empire to British trade and emigration. One politician should argue in support of the view that the empire is the most important part of British trade. The other politician should oppose this view.

Check your progress

I can describe some patterns of British trade.
I can explain why the empire was important for British trade.
I can assess the role of the empire in trade and emigration.

The Scramble for Africa

In 1880 Europeans looked upon Africa as 'the Dark Continent'. Although Europeans had traded with Africa for hundreds of years, European settlement was limited mainly to the coasts of West and South Africa. By 1914 all of Africa except Ethiopia and Liberia were under European control. Why did European *colonisation* happen so suddenly? The process is called 'the Scramble for Africa' because it took place so fast. The scramble involved Britain, France, Germany, Portugal, Spain and Italy.

Getting you thinking

The pie chart shows the percentages of Africa's land area that European countries had acquired by 1914.

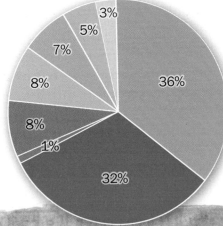

French	Belgian	
British	Portuguese	
Spanish	Italian	
German	Independent	

The cartoon shows European countries fighting over Africa. The figure on the left of the man depicting Africa, in a red uniform, represents Britain

Reasons for the Scramble for Africa

Trade

One of the earliest reasons for European interest in Africa was trade. Until the mid-19th century Europeans were interested in acquiring slaves. Many European countries, such as Britain and Germany, hoped that Africa would be a good place to sell their manufactured goods.

Settlement

Some Europeans hoped Africa would be a good place to settle. Before 1880, large numbers of Dutch speakers – known as Afrikaners – had created their own countries in southern Africa.

Precious metals

Settlers were also in search of gold, silver and other precious metals. Ghana, in west Africa, used to be called the Gold Coast. The search for raw materials was an important reason for European interest in acquiring African territories. Many attempts to find large amounts of precious metals failed. The world's greatest reserves of diamonds and gold, however, were discovered in South Africa. This encouraged Britain to acquire colonies in southern Africa.

The search for glory

The French army aimed to win glory by conquering lands in west and central Africa. This helped create a large colonial empire for France by 1914. In its search for military glory, Italy acquired Libya in north Africa in 1912.

Acquiring personal wealth

Many Europeans hoped to become wealthy by acquiring land in Africa. King Leopold of Belgium created a vast personal empire in the Congo area. In South Africa, the British businessman Cecil Rhodes became a millionaire through diamond mining. He also wanted to increase his wealth by acquiring gold mines. He persuaded Britain to acquire the area of Africa now known as Zimbabwe and Zambia.

Fear of losing out

What turned a search for land into a scramble was a country's fear that other European nations would take land and it would be left out. This helps explain the speed of the event.

Protecting the Suez Canal

The Suez Canal was the main sea route from Europe to Asia. Britain occupied Egypt as a way to make sure its shipping to India and Australia was protected.

Spreading Christianity

French and British missionaries helped persuade their countries to acquire land as a way of spreading Christianity.

Now it's your turn

1 Study the reasons above. Make a table, placing the reasons under the following headings: Economic reasons; Political reasons; Military reasons; Other reasons.
2 What do you regard as the two most important reasons why the Scramble for Africa took place?

Check your progress

I can describe reasons why the Scramble took place.

I can identify different types of reasons.

I can decide on the most important reasons, and say why.

The South African War

Objectives

By the end of the lesson you will be able to:

- explain why the South African War was a significant historical event
- explain the impact of the South African War on Britain and its position in the world

Getting you thinking

The photograph shows British troops in the South African War. It lasted from 1899 to 1902. For three years, the might of the British Army fought the farmers of two Dutch-speaking republics, the Transvaal and the Orange Free State. At stake was control of the world's greatest reserves of gold and of the whole of southern Africa. In the end Britain won the war, but it had a major impact on Britain's position in the world and on Britain itself.

Britain wanted to control all of southern Africa. The Cape of Good Hope at the southern tip of Africa controlled a major shipping route for Britain. Inland in southern Africa some of the richest deposits of diamonds and gold had been discovered. Britain feared that if it did not control this area, other countries such as Germany might acquire it.

Soldiers defending a strongpoint in the South African War, 1900

Unfortunately for Britain, the land containing most of the gold was in the hands of Dutch-speaking farmers who had created two states: the Transvaal and the Orange Free State. By 1899 Britain was determined to take control, even to the point of going to war. The British government was confident that any war would be swift and short. The Dutch-speaking farmers, known as Boers, would be no match for Britain's army. The British were in for a big surprise!

In October 1899 the Boers attacked and defeated British forces in southern Africa and surrounded important towns including Mafeking and Ladysmith. Britain had to send thousands of extra troops to fight the Boers. By 1900 Britain occupied most of the Boer lands. Then the Boers changed military tactics. They started hit-and-run raids against British troops. Only after two more bitter years of fighting did the Boers give up. By that time Britain had lost 40,000 troops.

The war was a humiliation for Britain even though it had won. The British Army had been out-fought by a much smaller army of volunteers. Moreover, Britain's way of defeating the Boers created hostility around the world. Boer women and children were forced into concentration camps, where thousands died of starvation.

The war was a shock to Britain for other reasons. Thousands of men who volunteered to fight in the British army were turned away because of their poor physical condition. After the war the government began introducing reforms to improve the physical condition of children. Free school meals, medical inspection of school children and more physical exercise in school were introduced. A British general, Lord Baden-Powell, founded the Boy Scouts movement, to encourage British boys to take part in outdoor exercise, and learn about military discipline – which would help prepare them to fight in a possible future war.

At the height of the South African War, Britain felt isolated, as other countries criticised British tactics. After the war Britain looked for allies. In 1902 Britain made an international agreement with Japan, and, in 1904, with France.

Now it's your turn APP

You are a journalist who has gone to report on the South African War. You have to persuade your newspaper that your story on what is happening should be on the front page. Using the information above, write an article for your newspaper that contains a headline and four major reasons which explain the war's importance.

Check your progress

I can describe the main events of the war.
I can explain the impact of the war on Britain.
I can say why the war was a significant historical event.

The Amritsar Massacre, 1919

Objectives

At the end of the lesson you will be able to:

- explain the events of the Amritsar massacre
- explain why it was an important event in Indian history

By 1919 a growing number of Indian nationalists wanted Britain to give them self-government within the British Empire. Many of these nationalists were members of the Indian National Congress. Its leaders, such as Nehru and Jinnah, all hoped to persuade the British to give Indians new rights. However, one leader, Mahatma Gandhi, wanted to force the British to change their views. He suggested civil disobedience. This was non-violent protest against British rule. This would involve peaceful demonstrations and *strikes*.

Getting you thinking

In 1919, serious rioting broke out all over the province of Punjab in north west India.

On 10 April at Amritsar, the holy city of the Sikh religion, the British arrested two Indian nationalist leaders. A large crowd of Indians attempted to get into the British area of the city but were turned back by police. The crowd began rioting in the city. As a result of the rioting, General Dyer, the British general in charge, banned all public meetings. He hoped this would restore order.

On 13 April an illegal meeting took place in the middle of the city, in a large open space called Jallianwalla Bagh. The crowd were unarmed and contained many women and children.

When Dyer heard about this, he went with 90 Gurkha and Indian troops and two armoured cars to Jallianwalla Bagh. He made sure that his troops blocked all possible escape routes. Without warning he ordered his troops to fire on the unarmed crowd. They fired 1,605 bullets. This resulted in 379 dead and 1,200 wounded among the crowd.

On 14 April another riot took place. This time the British used aircraft to machine-gun the rioters.

From 15 April to 9 June, Dyer introduced martial law. During that period Indians were forced by troops to walk on all fours past a spot where a British missionary woman had been attacked.

In October the British set up an inquiry into the massacre. It contained four British and four Indian officials. General Dyer was criticised. He was removed from command. His actions were supported in Britain where a newspaper raised £26,000 for Dyer. Dyer never apologised for his actions. At the inquiry Dyer said:

Strike: refusing to work, to put pressure on an employer or government

The Amritsar Massacre

'I fired and continued to fire until the crowd dispersed. I consider the amount of firing would produce the right effect to allow me to do my duty. If more troops were at hand the casualties would have been greater. It was no longer a question of dispersing the crowd but one of producing an effect on all of the Punjab.'

At the end of 1919 the British introduced reforms that allowed Indians more say in the government of India.

Now it's your turn

1 Describe the events that led to the Amritsar massacre.
2 Do you think General Dyer's actions can be justified? Give reasons for your answer.
3 Why do you think the Amritsar massacre was such an important event in Indian history?

Check your progress

I can describe events leading up to the Amritsar massacre.
I can explain why it is regarded as a significant historical event.
I can assess the role of General Dyer in the events of the massacre.

Gandhi, and the campaign for India's independence

Objectives

At the end of the lesson you will be able to:

- describe major events in Gandhi's life
- explain Gandhi's role in the campaign for Indian independence

Getting you thinking

Look at the photograph. It shows Gandhi surrounded by a group of supporters. He has a shaven head and is wearing a simple cotton robe and wears sandals. These are the clothes of a poor Indian farmer. This was deliberate. Although born into a wealthy family and educated at Cambridge University in England, Gandhi became the leader of Indian demands for independence from Britain.

More than any other person, Gandhi can be called the 'father of Indian independence'.

As a young lawyer Gandhi's life reached a turning point. He went to South Africa where he experienced, first-hand, racial discrimination against Indians by white settlers. Asians were treated as second-class citizens. Gandhi led a campaign to win equal rights for Indians. In doing so he developed tactics that he followed all his life. He was a supporter of non-violent protest.

Gandhi's tactics were so effective that the white-dominated South African government was forced to give Indians more rights.

Gandhi and his supporters, on the 'salt march' against British rule

In 1915 Gandhi returned to India. By this time, he had abandoned his western clothes and began to dress like an ordinary Indian farmer. The well-educated leaders of the Indian National Congress looked down on Gandhi.

However, Gandhi's support for non-violent protest won over these leaders. From 1919 to 1921, an India-wide campaign of strikes and demonstrations brought India to a standstill. The British in India seemed unable to stop it.

By 1921 Gandhi had become the leader of India's campaign for self-government. His simple dress and his non-violence impressed fellow Indians and people around the world. A small, humble man with nothing more than a walking stick and simple clothing was threatening the might of the world's largest empire.

In 1930 he was invited to London to meet the king and prime minister. Back in India, Gandhi continued to fight British rule. He led a salt march across India to the sea as a protest against British taxes on salt. It was a great success.

During his career the British arrested Gandhi many times and placed him in prison. At no time did he protest. His quiet manner inspired other Indians to break the law and fill India's prisons.

On 15 August 1947, Gandhi achieved part of his dream when India became independent. Despite Gandhi's efforts to prevent this, however, British India was divided into two states, India and Pakistan. In January 1948, while on his way to prayers, Gandhi was murdered by an extremist of his own Hindu faith.

Some historians argue that, without Gandhi, India would not have achieved independence in 1947.

Gandhi's methods were adopted by others. Martin Luther King, the African American civil rights leader, used Gandhi's methods to gain civil rights for black Americans in the 1950s and 1960s.

Now it's your turn

Create a timeline of the main events of Gandhi's life, showing the significance of his ideas and actions.

Check your progress

I can describe the main events of Gandhi's life.
I can explain Gandhi's role in the Indian independence movement.
I can assess Gandhi's role as a significant person in history.

The partition of India

Getting you thinking

At midnight on 14 August 1947, the British flag was lowered for the last time over its Indian empire. The following day two new countries came into being: India and Pakistan. Why was British India split into two countries?

Indian nationalists, such as *Nehru*, wanted to see one independent country to replace Britain's rule in India. The religious, cultural and political divisions in India made this task very difficult.

How diverse was India?

Religion

India was a land of many religions, the largest of which was Hinduism. However, there were other major religions. Many Indians were followers of Islam; the majority of Muslims lived in north-west India or Bengal, but they were found all over India. Sikhs were found mainly in the Punjab province of north-west India, but also, like Muslims, they lived across India. There were also Jains, Christians and Buddhists.

Language

India had almost 50 major languages. Although Hindi was the main language, there were many others. The only language spoken across India was English!

Indian states

Not all of India was under British rule. There were hundreds of Indian native states. These were ruled by an Indian ruler such as a maharaja or prince. Some states were tiny, others were very large – even as big as Britain.

These states were independent. If a united independent India was to be set up, these rulers had to agree.

Regional differences

India is a *sub-continent*. It contains different climate zones, which include mountains, deserts, forests and plains.

How was India partitioned in 1947?

After World War Two the British decided to leave India. But to whom would they hand over power? Gandhi wanted to see one Indian state.

Not all Indians wanted this. Mohammed Ali Jinnah led the Muslim League. He wanted a separate Muslim state. When handing over power, Britain had to deal with both the Indian National Congress and the Muslim League.

Nehru: India's first prime minister and supporter of a united India
Viceroy: representative of the British king

The last viceroy, Lord Mountbatten, sitting with Nehru, Jinnah and other Indian leaders in 1947

The British appointed Lord Mountbatten, in 1947, to hand over power in India. He was Britain's last *viceroy*. Mountbatten wanted to prevent violence between Hindus and Muslims. He believed the best way to stop the fighting was to divide India into two. One country would be mainly Hindu, the other mainly Muslim. Where would the border be between these new states?

Mountbatten created a Muslim state in two parts, divided by hundreds of miles. In north-west India, he created West Pakistan; in eastern India, East Pakistan, which today is the country of Bangladesh.

As August 1947 approached, millions of people – Hindu and Muslim – crossed northern India. They wanted to be in a country made up of the majority of their own religion. This was one of the biggest movements of people in history.

After the British left, there was violence between Muslims and Hindus. Tens of thousands died. In 1948 India and Pakistan went to war because each wanted to acquire Kashmir. Since that time India and Pakistan have gone to war with each other three times.

Now it's your turn

1   Find a partner. You have been asked to debate what should happen to India after the British leave. One will support Nehru's point of view: they should create an independent, united India. The other will support Jinnah's view: they should partition India and create an independent Pakistan.
2   Write short statements in support of your view, then read these out to the rest of the class. Ask them to vote in favour of one side or the other.

Check your progress

☆   I can describe events leading to the partition of India.
☆☆   I can explain why partition took place.
☆☆☆ I can assess the historical consequences of partition.

Sub-continent: a vast area of land

The growth of the Commonwealth

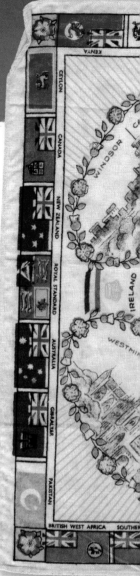

Objectives

By the end of the lesson you will be able to:

- describe how the Commonwealth came into being
- explain why the Commonwealth has survived

Look at the picture. It shows a souvenir towel from Queen Elizabeth II's coronation, with the queen surrounded by drawings of royal buildings, and the flags of all the Commonwealth countries. By 1953, when the coronation took place, these countries were all independent. But in the mid–19th century, they were all part of the British Empire, and governed from London. How did it change?

Getting you thinking

The Commonwealth has replaced the British Empire. In the 19th century Britain had colonies on every continent. It became very difficult for Britain to rule such a large and diverse empire.

The beginnings of change came when areas in which British settlers lived wanted more say in how they were governed. Like Britain, they wanted the right to vote and to choose their own parliament and government.

The British government feared another American War of Independence. It also supported the idea of local self-government because it reduced the costs of running the empire. Self-governing areas paid for their own government.

From the 1850s New Zealand received self-government. In 1867 Britain created the Dominion of Canada, and in 1900 the Commonwealth of Australia.

Each of these countries had something in common. They were areas of white settlement and were also thousands of miles from Britain.

By the end of the First World War in 1918, the British Empire was made up of two kinds of territories: the self-governing *white dominions* and the non-white colonies which were ruled from London.

In 1931 all the white dominions were given complete control over their own affairs, as long as they recognised the British monarch as their head of state. These dominions were known as the Commonwealth.

White dominions: self-governing parts of the British Empire before 1947

A souvenir towel from the coronation of Queen Elizabeth II, 1953

A big change came in 1947 when India and Pakistan became independent. They joined the Commonwealth. From that date onwards the Commonwealth became a multi-racial organisation.

Most countries that received independence from the British Empire joined the Commonwealth. They shared a common history and took part in their own international sports competition called the Commonwealth Games.

All Commonwealth countries agreed two fundamental ideas. One was the idea of democratic government. The other was anti-racism. In 1961 South Africa was thrown out of the Commonwealth because of its racist policies against non-whites. Fiji and Pakistan have both been thrown out of the Commonwealth when they have had military dictatorships. Also, all members of the Commonwealth regard the Queen of England as their head of state. Apart from the Commonwealth Games, Commonwealth prime ministers have regular meetings to discuss matters of common interest.

Today the Commonwealth is an important organisation that helps unite countries across the world – rich and poor, European, African and Asian.

Now it's your turn

You are a reporter for a British TV company at the 2010 Commonwealth Games in India. You are asked to give a five-minute report explaining the history and importance of the Commonwealth.

Write your report from the information in this lesson and give your report to the class.

Check your progress

I can describe how the Commonwealth developed.
I can identify how the Commonwealth changed over time.
I can identify change and continuity in the growth of the Commonwealth.

The end of empire

Objectives

By the end of the lesson you will be able to:

- explain why Britain lost its empire

- describe how Britain's colonies won their independence

Getting you thinking

Look at the photograph. It shows the British flag being lowered for the last time in Kenya, a former African colony of the British Empire. This event happened across the world in the 20 years after World War Two. In 1945 Britain had the world's largest empire. By 1970 it had all but disappeared.

The Union Jack is lowered for the last time in Nairobi, Kenya, in 1963

In 1945 Britain had won World War Two. It had gone to war to protect the British Empire. However, in the decades after the war Britain allowed most of its former colonies to gain independence. There is a number of reasons why Britain gave up its colonies.

Opposition to British rule in its empire

All over the empire, people under British rule wanted to rule themselves. The most important part of the empire was the British Indian Empire. Here the Indian National Congress and the Muslim League wanted independence. They led demonstrations and organised strikes in an attempt to force Britain to leave. From 1918 Britain gave Indians a bigger and bigger role in governing India. Finally, in 1947, Britain decided to leave. In its place two new countries were created: India and Pakistan.

These events were repeated across the empire. In Africa, Asia and the West Indies, local people wanted to rule themselves. In some colonies opposition to British rule was violent. In Kenya, in Africa, a rebellion took place in the 1950s called the Mau Mau rebellion. In Malaya, in Asia, an uprising by communists began in 1948. However, in most colonies the changeover to independence was peaceful, with Britain handing over *democratic* government to the local population.

The cost of empire

Fighting World War Two had cost Britain lots of money. By 1945 Britain was almost bankrupt. It had to ask the USA for huge loans. The cost of keeping armed forces stationed across the empire was becoming too expensive. Britain simply could not afford to keep its empire.

Also, from 1945 Britain was involved in the cold war. This was a confrontation between the USA and Britain against the Union of Soviet Socialist Republics (USSR). This meant that most of the British armed forces were based in central Europe to prevent an attack by the USSR on Germany.

The creation of the Commonwealth

When Britain gave independence to its former colonies it encouraged them to join the Commonwealth of Nations. This organisation had the British monarch as its head. This meant Britain could keep close links with these new countries.

Now it's your turn

Two people are having a debate about Britain's empire. One wants to keep it. The other wants to give the colonies independence.
1   In pairs or small groups write down reasons to support each side of the debate.
2   As a class compile your reasons and decide who you think put forward the strongest case.

Check your progress

I can explain how and when Britain lost its empire.
I can explain reasons for the loss of empire.
I can assess the importance of the different reasons.

Massacre at Sharpeville, 1960

Objectives

By the end of the lesson you will be able to

- describe how non-white people in South Africa were denied freedom

- explain why the events at Sharpeville were an important historical event

South Africa was a member of the Commonwealth in 1945. Its government was controlled by the white population, even though most people were black. In 1948 this government introduced new laws that set up 'apartheid'. This word means 'keeping people apart'. Whites, blacks and Asians were forced to live in their own areas. They were forced to use separate train carriages, toilets, even benches in a park. This caused non-white people to protest.

Getting you thinking

In South Africa non-white people were forced to carry passbooks. This showed a person's name and address. At any time police could ask to see their passbook. Non-white South Africans found this humiliating.

The Sharpeville Massacre, 1960

Townships: temporary towns where non-whites were forced to live by the apartheid government

Many decided to protest. On 21 March 1960, a crowd of approximately 5,000 unarmed black people went to a police station in Sharpeville, a black *township*. They wanted to protest against passbooks. They hoped the white government would get rid of them.

At 10.00 in the morning a large crowd were outside the police station. Inside were 20 policemen. The South African army used jet fighters to fly low over the crowd to frighten them. The police from outside Sharpeville turned up in an armoured car.

At 1.15 pm the police opened fire. They killed 69 unarmed protestors, including eight women and ten children. Over 180 were injured. The police said some of the crowd had thrown stones at them. The white commander of the police, Colonel Pienaar, said his policemen were in danger and he feared violence.

The events at Sharpeville caused uproar. Demonstrations against the white government took place across South Africa. The government arrested and imprisoned over 18,000 people.

Countries in the Commonwealth were outraged and protested. South Africa was forced out of the Commonwealth. From 1961 Commonwealth countries began to boycott South Africa. They refused to buy South African goods. They also refused to play sport with South Africa until apartheid was ended.

Inside South Africa the massacre changed the views of many protestors. Before the Sharpeville Massacre Nelson Mandela, a leader of the *African National Congress*, hoped to use peaceful ways to persuade the white government to end apartheid. After the massacre he believed that the only way to get rid of white rule was by violence. He supported attacks on government forces. He was arrested and given life imprisonment. Although in prison, Nelson Mandela became a symbol of the fight of non-white South Africans for equal rights. He was eventually released in 1990. He helped end apartheid and became South Africa's first black president.

Now it's your turn

1 A turning point in history is an event that brings about important changes. In what ways was the Sharpeville Massacre of 1960 a turning point in the history of South Africa?
2 Using the evidence above, write a short report on the Sharpeville Massacre showing why you think it was an important historical event.

Check your progress

I can describe the events at Sharpeville.
I can explain why Sharpeville was an important historical event.
I can explain why Sharpeville was a turning point in South Africa's history.

African National Congress: *an organisation that wanted equality for all people in South Africa*

Immigration to Britain

Objectives

y the end of the
esson you will be
ble to

describe how
people came to
migrate to Britain

explain reasons for
immigration to
Britain

Today Britain is a multicultural country. The country is home to people from many ethnic backgrounds, religions and cultures. Many of these people are descended from immigrants who arrived in Britain after World War Two. Why do you think they travelled across the world to find a new home in Britain?

Getting you thinking

When trying to explain why people decide to leave one country to settle in another, we sometimes refer to 'push' reasons and 'pull' reasons. 'Pull' reasons refer to why people are attracted towards something. 'Push' reasons refer to why people are forced away from something.

'Pull' reasons

Looking for a better life

Look at the photograph. It shows a ship called the *Empire Windrush*. It is famous because, in 1948, it brought the first West Indians to Britain after World War Two. Most of the West Indian immigrants were young men, who came looking for work. Britain offered the opportunity for higher wages and a better standard of living than they had experienced in the West Indies. Also Britain was short of workers after the war. Organisations such as London Transport had a campaign in the West Indies to encourage workers to come to Britain.

Since the arrival of the *Empire Windrush,* many people from around the world have decided to come to Britain to seek a better standard of living. For most of the period since 1945 Britain has been one of the world's wealthiest countries. It has offered lots of opportunities for those looking for work. Most of the immigrants until the 1990s came from Commonwealth countries. These people had the right to work and live in Britain, which was denied to people from outside the Commonwealth. This included people from India, Pakistan, Australia and New Zealand.

From the 1990s onwards, other people came to Britain from within the European Union. These included people from Portugal, and, after 2004, from Poland and the Baltic States. They all had the right to live and work in a country which offered higher wages than their homeland.

People were also attracted to Britain because it is a democracy, with equal civil rights for all its citizens.

'Push' reasons

Fleeing persecution

Many people came to Britain to escape persecution in their own lands. Before World War Two, many thousands of Jews fled their homes in Germany because they faced violence and even death.

Since 1945 many other groups of people have come to Britain for similar reasons. In 1971 Asians were expelled from Uganda by the dictator, Idi Amin, and Britain offered Ugandan Asians a new home. Many people have fled to Britain because of war. Africans from Congo, Rwanda and Somalia have come to Britain because it offers safety.

Famine

Some people were forced to flee their homelands because of famine and drought. Somalis and Ethiopians suffered a terrible famine in the 1980s.

Now it's your turn

Make a 1940s poster for London Transport that provides reasons why people in the West Indies ought to emigrate to Britain.

Check your progress

I can describe some of the different nationalities who have come to live in Britain since World War Two.

I can explain reasons why people have migrated to Britain.

I can describe both 'push' and 'pull' reasons for immigration.

End of empire: Britain in 2010

Signs on a London street show the diversity of modern-day Britain

Getting you thinking

One of the greatest athletes Britain has produced since World War Two is Linford Christie. He is the only man to win a gold medal in the 100 metres at the Olympics, European, Commonwealth and World Championships. He was born in Jamaica and raised in Britain. He is just one of hundreds of thousands of people from the former British Empire, who have made an important contribution to British life.

Multicultural Britain

Look at the photograph of a typical street in a modern-day British city. It shows shops owned and run by people from a wide variety of ethnic groups. This is an example of how the empire has had a major impact on British life. After World War Two people from across the British Empire were given the right to settle in Britain. Many came from areas such as the West Indies and India and Pakistan. This has brought many changes to life in Britain.

In a newspaper survey in 2003, it was announced that the most popular food in Britain was chicken tikka masala, a mix of Indian and British cookery. The meal is unique to Britain and was created by British Asians. In the Football World Cup of 2006, the English team included players who are descendants of people from across the old empire and Commonwealth, such as Wayne Rooney (Ireland), Owen Hargreaves (Canada), and Sol Campbell (Jamaica).

Remnants of empire

Britain still has a small number of colonies overseas, which it still has to defend. These are usually islands that are so small they would find it difficult to form an independent country. These include the Falkland Islands in the South Atlantic. Argentina claims the Falklands as part of its own territory, and went to war with Britain in 1982 to try to take them. Other British colonies include Bermuda, Gibraltar, Ascension Island and the islands of St Helena and Montserrat.

Look at an atlas to see where these last *remnants* of empire are located.

Trade

Britain is now a member of the European Union. However, it still keeps strong trade links with parts of the former empire and Commonwealth. New Zealand butter and lamb, Australian wine and South African apples are all examples of how trade with countries of the former British Empire shapes life in today's Britain.

Local history

In 1951 a census took place. The vast majority of the population said they were Christian. Since that time Britain has became a land of many religions. Towns and cities now contain religious buildings for the following faiths:

church/chapels	for Christians
mosques	for Muslims
gurdwaras	for Sikhs
temples	for Hindus
synagogues	for Jews

Now it's your turn

1 In what ways has Britain become multicultural?
2 Produce a poster showing Britain as a multicultural country.

Extension work

Look around your own local town or city to see if you can spot the buildings of different religious faiths.

Check your progress

I can describe how the empire has shaped today's Britain.
I can use photographs and other sources as evidence of multiculturalism.
I can give examples of how British culture has been influence by immigration.

Remnant: small piece

The British Empire: change over time

The cover of the *Sydney Mail*, September 16, 1914

In unit 5 you have examined how Britain's empire developed, and its impact on Britain and the peoples it governed overseas. You have also looked at some of the most significant events in the history of the British Empire in the 19th and 20th centuries. In this lesson you are going to look at the idea of change over time. This means thinking about how events over time connect with each other.

Getting you thinking

The image shows the front page of an Australian newspaper during the First World War. It shows the British lion sitting on the British flag with Australian soldiers in the background.

What message do you think this picture is trying to convey?

During the early 20th century there were many changes in the British Empire. Many parts of the empire became self-governing. One of these was Australia. Eventually most of the empire became independent. By the late 20th century, the empire had been replaced by the Commonwealth.

Britain itself was also changing. Many people from the empire and Commonwealth came to live in Britain, turning it into a multicultural society.

Activity 1

During the period 1900–2010 many changes took place in Britain's position in the world. Create a timeline of the major changes and events, using evidence from this unit. What events will you include on the timeline, and what will you miss out?

Activity 2

It is important in history to find links between historical events.

From your study of unit 5, can you identify events that linked together to cause changes in the British Empire? Create a mind map entitled *Why did the British Empire end?*, with lines showing how different historical events are linked.

Now it's your turn

Britain has changed in many ways since 1900, but some things may have stayed the same. Look for examples of *continuity* in the following areas:
- how Britain is governed
- Britain's relations with the rest of the world
- how people live, and the kinds of jobs they do

1 Write a short report, answering the question: *What has stayed the same in Britain over the past 100 years?* Include a series of headings covering different themes.
2 Britain's place in the world is very different in 2010 from 1900. Can you sum up in two sentences the main ways in which Britain's place in the world has changed?

Check your progress

I can describe some key changes that have occurred over the past 110 years.

I can give reasons for the changes that have occurred.

I can show how some of these changes are linked.

What was the greatest invention of the 19th century?

Objectives

By the end of this lesson you will be able to

- describe some 19th-century inventions
- make a judgement on what you think was the most important invention

The 19th century was a period of rapid change. In 1800, if you wished to travel from Manchester to London it would take you several days. By 1860 it took only a few hours, after horse-drawn travel was replaced by railway travel. The railways transformed Britain: newspapers printed in London at 9.00pm at night could be read the next morning in cities such as Liverpool, Glasgow and Birmingham. People could now live miles from work and travel by train. This led to the growth of suburbs around towns. Food and manufactured goods could be transported in large quantities quickly and cheaply. The steam locomotive is one contender for the greatest invention of the 19th century.

The machinery hall in the Great Exhibition of 1851

The age of inventions

Building London's sewer system

Blueprint of a steam locomotive

An operating theatre in the 1890s

Getting you thinking

Britain in the 19th century went through what historians call the Industrial Revolution. In 1800 most people in Britain lived in villages and small towns; most people worked in agriculture. By 1900, most people lived in cities and large towns, and were employed in industry.

These extraordinary changes were brought about, in part, by new inventions. The mass production of cotton cloth, for example, was only made possible by the invention of mechanised spinning machines in the late 18th century. Where once it took one person a week to produce two metres of cotton cloth, the same amount could now be made in under one hour.

Now it's your turn 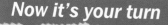 APP

Here is a timeline of inventions from the 19th century.

1 Using the internet, find out about how each invention affected life in Britain.
2 Using the list of inventions mentioned above decide which ones:
   a improved the quality of people's lives
   b improved industry
   c made life more dangerous
3 Give a five-minute talk to your class about what you think is the greatest invention of the 19th century. Choose an invention (other than the steam locomotive!), explain what it was, how it affected life in Britain, and why you think it was the most important. You may wish to choose something not on the list, such as the invention of antiseptics and anaesthesia in medicine.

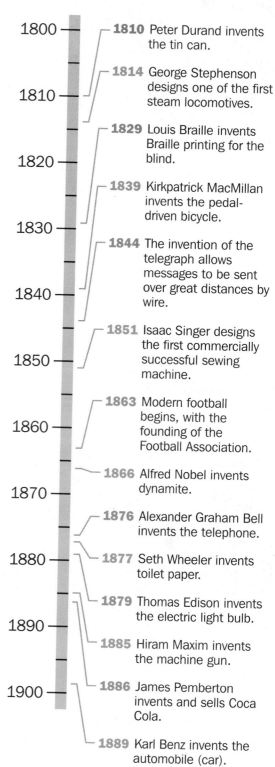

1800
1810 **1810** Peter Durand invents the tin can.
1814 George Stephenson designs one of the first steam locomotives.
1829 Louis Braille invents Braille printing for the blind.
1820 **1839** Kirkpatrick MacMillan invents the pedal-driven bicycle.
1830 **1844** The invention of the telegraph allows messages to be sent over great distances by wire.
1840
1851 Isaac Singer designs the first commercially successful sewing machine.
1850
1863 Modern football begins, with the founding of the Football Association.
1860
1866 Alfred Nobel invents dynamite.
1870 **1876** Alexander Graham Bell invents the telephone.
1880 **1877** Seth Wheeler invents toilet paper.
1879 Thomas Edison invents the electric light bulb.
1890 **1885** Hiram Maxim invents the machine gun.
1900 **1886** James Pemberton invents and sells Coca Cola.
1889 Karl Benz invents the automobile (car).

Check your progress

I can describe some inventions of the 19th century.
I can explain how inventions changed life in the 19th century.
I can make a judgement on which invention was most important, and give reasons.

Why was change so rapid in 19th-century Britain?

Objectives

By the end of this lesson you will be able to:

- describe some changes in 19th-century Britain
- identify and explain the most important changes to Britain during the 19th century

New inventions, medical advancements, improved transport and various individuals all caused rapid change in Britain in the 19th century.

Getting you thinking

In what different ways do you think the development of steam railways changed the lives of people in 19th-century Britain?

Steam engines revolutionised transport in the 19th century. In 1781 James Watt designed a steam engine that could turn a wheel. In the 19th century this new technology led to the creation of steam trains and steam ships. People and goods could be transported around Britain more cheaply and quickly. People could then buy cheaper goods and had more opportunities to travel.

A train on the Liverpool and Manchester Railway

Bacteria: organisms which cause disease and can only be seen through a microscope

The railways and steam locomotives of the 19th century needed huge amounts of iron, steel, building materials, coal. New inventions met these increased demands. In 1839 James Nasmyth invented the steam hammer, which could produce huge sheets of iron to make ships and bridges. Henry Bessemer designed a new 'convertor', which produced steel more cheaply and in larger quantities.

Demand for coal increased in the 19th century. Expanding cities and a rising population led to greater demand for coal to heat people's houses. Coal was needed to power steam trains and to make coal gas for street lighting. In 1750, five million tonnes of coal were produced. By 1850, this had risen to 49.4 million tonnes.

In the 19th century young children worked in terrible conditions in factories and mines. Children aged as young as six worked 12-15 hour days, Monday to Saturday. Public pressure grew on British governments to prevent the exploitation of children and women. British governments passed different acts to improve working conditions. In 1878 the Factory and Workshops Act was passed. Women were limited to working 56.5 hours in textile factories. Factories were barred from employing children under 10 years old. Later in the 19th century educational opportunities began to improve for children. In 1870 the Elementary Education Act was passed; this resulted in many more people being able to read and write by the end of the 19th century.

The growth of factories in the 19th century brought more people into the cities. Improvements were made to public health through sanitation, and advances in medical knowledge. Louis Pasteur, in 1864, proved that *bacteria* caused diseases. In 1875 the Sale of Food and Drugs Act set out rules against bad food being sold. Workers in the cities became more organised and trade unions were established. The Trade Union Act of 1871 recognised that trade unions had legal rights. Improved agricultural techniques, such as better fertilisers, meant enough food was produced to feed the growing population of Britain.

Now it's your turn

Was steam power the most important reason for rapid change in the 19th century? You will need to compare the impact of steam power to other changes, such as improved educational opportunities.

Check your progress

I can describe some key changes in Britain in the 19th century.
I can explain why these changes took place during the 19th century.
I can explain how developments in one field led to other new inventions, and give examples.

What were the major changes affecting Britain from 1750 to 2010?

Britain in the period 1750–2010 experienced many changes. Technological advancements in transport and industry transformed Britain. Political changes occurred that caused the growth and the decline of the British Empire and changed the lives of many people across the globe.

Historians have different opinions on what they think were the most important changes that affected Britain in this period. Now it's your turn to judge what you think are the most important changes.

Immigrants to the UK attend a ceremony to become British citizens

Chronological: starting with the earliest event and following the order in which events occurred

Assessment task

You are going to write a magazine article called 'Important moments in British history' showing what you think are the most significant events in British history between 1750 and 2010.

These might be political events, new inventions, medical advances, or social changes. Your article should be *chronological*, and include no more than ten examples. You can use images or drawings to illustrate the events. You should include an explanation informing the reader why you think each event is important and how it links with other events or changes.

Before you write your article:
- make a list of any events that you think are important
- think about why they are important, how many people they affected, and whether their effects were lasting
- narrow your list down to those events that you think have had the greatest impact
- think about your reader – which events do you think will be most interesting for them to read about?
- look through the images in this unit. Which ones could you use to illustrate why you think your events are important?

Check your level – have you?

I can name some important events and changes.	I can include people, events and changes in my article.	I can show knowledge of why these events were important
I can describe the importance of events and changes.	I can clearly describe the significance of these people, events and changes.	I can identify and explain connections between events and why they are important.
I can use some historical words in my article.	I can use historical terms in my article.	I can use historical terms and images to make my ideas clear and my article interesting.
Level **4**	Level **5**	Level **6**

Glossary

Abolition: the ending, in law, of a practice or tradition

Aborigines: the original inhabitants of Australia

Administrator: a person who helps run a country or organisation

African National Congress: an organisation that wanted equality for all people in South Africa

Arrogant: having an exaggerated opinion of your own importance

Assemblies: where people would meet to discuss and issue laws

Autobiography: a book written by a person about his or her own life

Bacteria: organisms which cause disease and can only be seen through a microscope

Bankrupt: no longer having money to pay debts

Borough: an area that sends MPs to parliament

Casualty: a person killed or wounded in a battle

Census: a survey of the population of a country or place, carried out every ten years in the United Kingdom

Century: one hundred years

Cesspit: a deep pit used to dispose of sewage or rubbish

Chartists: campaigners for political and social change in the mid-19th century

Cholera: an often fatal disease spread by bacteria in contaminated water

Chronological: starting with the earliest event and following the order in which events occurred

Civil rights: rights including the vote and free speech

Clan: A group of families with a common surname

Colliery: a coal mine

Colonial rulers: people who ruled the West Indies for the British

Colonisation: the process of acquiring colonies

Colony: an overseas territory in an empire

Congress: the parliament of the United States

Constitutional Convention: a meeting to decide how the country would be governed

Convicted: found guilty in a court of law

Corn Laws: A tax on foreign wheat imported into Britain

Court: an enclosed square surrounded by houses

Court: the powerful people who surrounded the king

Crop rotation: a system in which a field is planted with different crops in succession

Customs duty/tariff: a tax placed on imports

Decade: ten years

Democracy: rule by the majority

Dominion: a country within the British Empire, but with some independence

Emigrate: To leave one country and settle in another country

Emigration: leaving one country for another

Emperor: a man who rules an empire

Empire: a group of countries ruled by one powerful country

Enclosure: the fencing in of land for arable farming (growing crops) or for animal breeding

Enginewright: an engineer in charge of a coal mine

Eviction: The forceful removal of a person from their home or land

Famine: When food becomes extremely scarce and people die from starvation and disease

Free trade: removal of trading restrictions between countries

Freight: the transport of goods by train

Guerrilla warfare: Small groups of fighters who launch surprise attacks

Heir: the next in line to the throne

Highland: a region in the northwest of Scotland

Highlanders: Scots who live in northwest Scotland

Hogmanay: Scottish New Year

Home Rule: Ireland would rule itself from its own parliament but remain part of the British Empire

Home Secretary: member of the government responsible for law and order

House of Lords: one of the Houses of Parliament

Hurry: to pull coal in a cart underground from coalface to the lift shaft

Industrial Revolution: the rapid change to Britain's economy in the 18th and 19th centuries

Infiltrate: To join a group or organisation in order to find out information and destroy it

Investments: the use of money to buy companies

Jacobite: A Scottish rebel, named after the Latin word 'Jacobus' meaning James

Justices of the peace: officers who enforced the king's law

Kirk: the Scottish church

Laissez faire: A belief that the market should be allowed to run itself

Landlord: A person who lets land or property for profit

Legislation: the passing of new laws by parliament

Legumes: any plant of the pea family, used to improve the soil

Linoleum: (lino), a floor covering made from linseed oil and resin, that was widely used after 1860

Locomotive: a steam engine that moves along rails

Magistrate: local person responsible for law and order, sometimes known as a Justice of the Peace (JP)

Maoris: the native people of New Zealand

Maroons: escaped slaves who established their own communities

Martial Law: When military law is introduced

Martyr: A person who is killed for their beliefs

Massacre: The killing of a large group of people

Militant: using extreme tactics in support of a cause

Monasteries: places where monks live and follow a religious life

Money bill: A law which involves spending money for the country

Mortal sin: one which means the sinner will go to hell when they die

Mughal Empire: An Indian empire which ruled India before the British took control

Napoleonic Wars: fought by the British against Napoleon Bonaparte

Nationalist: a supporter of a country's independence

Nehru: India's first prime minister and supporter of a united India

New England: the 13 northern colonies

Parish: the area around a church

Parliament: The British parliament is where laws are passed

Parliamentary election: voting to decide who will be the members of parliament (MPs) who run the country

Partition: Division into different parts

Patent: a legal document that stops anyone else copying your ideas

Penal Laws: Harsh laws which the English used to control the Irish

Pension: a sum of money paid to a person who has retired from work

Period: a defined length of time, such as the Tudor period

Plantation of Ulster: Land given to English and Scottish settlers in Ireland

Plantation: a farm for the production of tropical crops, such as sugar cane

Poor rate: a local tax

Poor relief: money given to help the poor

Presbyterian: a follower of a branch of Protestantism

Privy: toilet

Protectionism: protecting British companies by restricting other countries' right to trade

Protestantism: a form of Christianity that rejected the Catholic Church

Quakers: A religious group which opposed violence

Raj: refers to British rule in India from 1858 to 1947

Rebel: In this case someone who uses violence to end the Union of Ireland and Great Britain

Reformation: A period of religious reform in the 16th century

Refractory: behaving in a way which breaks the workhouse rules

Refrigerated ships: ships with a cold preserved foodstuffs

Remnant: small piece

Repeal: to cancel an act of pa

Republic: government witho

Republican: Irish suppor

Revolutionary: Some political change, an

179

Royalists: supporters of Charles I during the Civil War

Rural: to do with the countryside

Sepoys: Indian troops who served in the British Army

Sikhs: members of an Indian religion

Slave trade: the international trade in slaves from West Africa to the Americas

Slavery: where people are bought and sold as property

Smallpox: a disease that causes fever and severe blisters

Strike: refusing to work, to put pressure on an employer or government

Sub-continent: a vast area of land

Suffrage: the right to vote

Suffragette: militant (more extreme) campaigner for women's right to vote

Suffragist: peaceful campaigner for women's right to vote

Terrorist: A person who uses violence to achieve their political aims

Textile industry: the making of woollen or cotton cloth on a large scale

Textiles: industry making woven cloth

Tithes: a tax paid to the church

Townships: temporary towns where non-whites were forced to live by the apartheid government

Trade triangle: trading system based on the buying and selling of slaves in the 18th century

Trading post: a place used for trading goods

_et: a Twitter message of just _0 characters, including _s and punctuation!

_pressive rule by one _group

Ulster: A province in the north of Ireland

Unanimous: with everyone in agreement

Vaccination: introduction of a virus into a person to provide protection against diseases

Viceroy: British ruler of India after 1857

White dominions: self-governing parts of the British Empire before 1947

Young Pretender: James Edward Stuart was called the 'Old Pretender'. His son was called the 'Young Pretender' or 'Bonnie Prince Charlie'

Index

Index

Index

Acknowledgements

The publishers gratefully acknowledge the permission granted to reproduce the copyright material in this book. While every effort has been made to trace and contact copyright holders, where this has not been possible the publishers will be pleased to make the necessary arrangements at the first opportunity.

p. 9 Amgueddfa Cymru, National Museum Wales; p. 10 The Granger Collection/TopFoto; p. 10 Topham/Fotomas; p. 12 The Art Archive; p. 14 The Granger Collection/TopFoto; p. 16 City of London/HIP/TopFoto; p. 18 Royal Commission on the Ancient and Historical Monuments of Scotland; p. 18 TopFoto; p. 20 English School; p. 22 The Granger Collection/TopFoto; p. 24 UK City Images/TopFoto; p. 26 The Granger Collection/TopFoto; p. 28 Mary Evans Picture Library; p. 28 The Art Archive; p. 30 The Art Archive/John Meek; p. 31 Data reproduced © Crown Copyright, material is reproduced with the permission of the National Archives; p. 32 Punch Limited/TopFoto; p. 34 John Snow, On the Mode of Communication of Cholera, John Churchill, London, England, 1855; p. 36 SSPL via Getty Images; p. 38 SSPL via Getty Images; p. 39 SSPL via Getty Images; p. 40 The Granger Collection/TopFoto; p. 41 The Granger Collection/TopFoto; p. 42 The Art Archive; p. 44 Manchester Art Gallery/The Bridgeman Art Library; p. 46 Getty Images; p. 48 TopFoto/Fotomas; p. 51 Collections of Newport Museum and Art Gallery; p. 52 The Granger Collection/TopFoto; p. 53 The Granger Collection/TopFoto; quotation from Emmeline Pankhurst, My Own Story, Greenwood Press, 1985; p. 54 Museum of London/HIP/TopFoto; p. 56 Public Record Office/HIP; p. 58 Mary Evans/Peter Higginbotham Collection; p. 59 Mary Evans/Peter Higginbotham Collection; p. 60 Time & Life Pictures/Getty Images; p. 62 Getty Images; p. 63 Getty Images; p. 64 The Granger Collection/TopFoto; p. 65 The Granger Collection/TopFoto; p. 66 English School (19th century)/The Illustrated London News Picture Library/The Bridgeman Art Library; p. 68 TopFoto; p. 69 Data reproduced © Crown Copyright, material is reproduced with the permission of DWP; p. 70 Daily Mirror/Mirropix; data reproduced © Crown Copyright, material is reproduced with the permission of the National Archives; p. 71 British Library; p. 72 The National Archives; p. 74 Hulton Archive; p. 76 Royal collection; p. 78 Parliamentary Archives, London; p. 80 The Granger Collection/TopFoto; p. 81 Topham Picturepoint/TopFoto; p. 83 Topham Picturepoint; p. 84 Culture and Sport Glasgow (Museums)/The Bridgeman Art Library; p. 86 Museum of London/HIP/Topfoto; p. 88 The Drambuie Collection/The Bridgeman Art Library; p. 91 TopFoto; p. 93 The Art Archive/Eileen Tweedy; p. 94 Getty Images; p. 95 The Granger Collection/TopFoto; p. 97 The Granger Collection/TopFoto; p. 98 Library of Congress; p. 100 The Granger Collection/TopFoto; p. 102 Getty Images; p. 104 The Granger Collection/TopFoto; p. 107 Topham Picturepoint; p. 109 The Art Archive/Biblioteca d'Ajuda Lisbon/Alfredo Dagli Orti; p. 110 Tim Graham/Getty Images; p. 111 Photri/TopFoto; p. 112 Private Collection/The Bridgeman Art Library; p. 115 Getty Images; p. 116 Michael Graham-Stewart/The Bridgeman Art Library; p. 118 The Art Archive/Musée des Arts Africains et Océaniens/Gianni Dagli Orti; p. 119 Getty Images; p. 120 The Granger Collection/TopFoto; p. 122 Balean/TopFoto; p. 124 The Granger Collection/TopFoto; p. 126 Extract from The British Empire 1815-1914, by Dr Frank McDonough, Hodder Education, 1994; p. 127 The British Library/HIP; p. 129 Private Collection/Ken Welsh/The Bridgeman Art Library; p. 130 The Granger Collection/TopFoto; p. 132 The Granger Collection/TopFoto; p. 134 The Art Archive/Library of Congress; p. 136 The Granger Collection/TopFoto; p. 138 The British Library/TopFoto; p. 140 The Art Archive/Bodleian Library Oxford; p. 142 World History Archive/TopFoto; p. 144 Topham Picturepoint; p. 147 Mitchell Library, State Library of NSW/The Bridgeman Art Library; p. 148 Balean/TopFoto; p. 149 Data from A History of Economic Change in England 1880-1939, by RS Sayers, OUP, 1967; data from Age of Empire, by E J Hosbawm, Sphere Books, 1987; p. 150 The Art Archive/Private Collection/Marc Charmet; p. 152 The Granger Collection/TopFoto; p. 155 Mary Evans Picture Library; p. 156 Ullstein bild/TopFoto; p. 159 Topham/AP/TopFoto; p. 160 Land Lost Content/HIP/TopFoto; p. 162 Topham/AP/TopFoto; p. 164 Topham Picturepoint/TopFoto; p. 167 TopFoto; p. 168 Getty Images; p. 170 The Art Archive; p. 172 Getty Images; p. 172 Getty Images; p. 172 SSPL via Getty Images; p. 172 Artmedia/HIP/TopFoto; p. 174 SSPL via Getty Images; p. 176 AFP/Getty Images